Strategies of Fantasy

Strategies of Fantasy

BRIAN ATTEBERY

Indiana University Press

BLOOMINGTON AND INDIANAPOLIS

The paper used in this publication meets the minimum requirements of American
National Standard for Information Sciences—Permanence of Paper for Printed
Library Materials, ANSI Z39.48-1984.

Manufactured in the United States of America

Library of Congress Cataloging-in-Publication Data

Attebery, Brian, date.
    Strategies of fantasy / Brian Attebery.
      p.   cm.
    Includes bibliographical references and index.
    ISBN 0-253-31070-9 (cloth)
    1. Fantastic fiction, American—History and criticism—Theory,
etc. 2. Fantastic fiction, English—history and criticism—Theory,
etc. 3. Fantastic literature—History and criticism—Theory, etc.
4. Postmodernism (Literature) I. Title.
PS374.F27A87 1992
813'.0876609—dc20   91-15884

  1 2 3 4 5 96 95 94 93 92

CONTENTS

Introduction

In the last few years the number of studies of fantastic literature has grown prodigiously. From a few pioneering attempts to define and delimit the field, such as W. R. Irwin's *The Game of the Impossible* (1976), the field has grown to include author studies, historical surveys, thematic analyses, and several essay collections and conference volumes. This proliferation indicates a growing academic interest in a body of literature that deliberately violates the generic conventions of realism, conventions that not too long ago were generally used as defining criteria for great or serious fiction.

Looking at this sizable and growing body of critical and scholarly work on the fantastic, one might be tempted to conclude that there is no need for further words on the subject, first, because the fantastic has now achieved proper recognition from the literary establishment and, second, because anything worth saying has been said. The first of these premises is easily disproved. Just ask a Henry James scholar to read Gene Wolfe, a writer of comparable skill and an equal love of indirection and ambiguity, and see what kind of response you get. A look through recent feminist literary theory may turn up references to Joanna Russ's criticism, but rarely will one find mention of her fantastic fiction. Though fine studies of fantasy have appeared in specialist journals like *Extrapolation* and the *Journal of the Fantastic in the Arts,* most literary periodicals seem either unaware of its existence or convinced of its unimportance.

The second premise, that the fantasy field has been sufficiently mapped and measured, is harder to answer. Such works as Stephen Prickett's *Victorian Fantasy* (1979), Tobin Siebers's *The Romantic Fantastic* (1984), and E. F. Bleiler's survey *Supernatural Fiction Writers* (1985) are excellent guides to the historical development of the field. C. N. Manlove's *Modern Fantasy* (1975) and *The Impulse of Fantasy Literature* (1983) offer careful critical readings of classic fantasy texts. Ann Swinfen's *In Defense of Fantasy* (1984) offers a useful typology. Kathryn Hume explores the relationship of the fantastic to realistic representation in *Fantasy and Mimesis* (1984). My own *The Fantasy Tradition in American Literature* (1980) traces the cultural roots of fantasy literature and especially its imitation and incorporation of elements from magical folk narratives. I certainly thought, after writing that study, that I had nothing further to say on the subject.

Yet here I am introducing another book on fantasy. Credit (or blame) must go to two bodies of texts that have appeared or come to general attention in the decade since *The Fantasy Tradition* was published. The first is a burst of exciting new fantasy that has not only given me much pleasure but also made me rethink the dimensions and properties of the genre. Hence much of the discussion in the following pages concerns relatively recent fiction, though older texts might profitably be reexamined for the characteristics foregrounded within the newer.

The second group of texts consists of theoretical studies of narrative itself. Gérard Genette's analysis of time, Seymour Chatman's redefinition of character, Bakhtin's belatedly influential theory of the dialogical nature of the novel, Hirsch and Abel's identification of primarily feminine patterns of narrative development, structural and post-structural modes of analysis—these and other theoretical enterprises have altered our understanding of the processes of generating and reading fictional texts. Thereby we have been granted new visions of the texts themselves. Many of these theories interact quite excitingly with fantasy texts. Much recent fantasy is, indeed, a product of the same ferment that spurred the theorizing, sometimes with the author's active and conscious intent (as is the case with Samuel Delany, Ursula K. Le Guin, or John Crowley) and sometimes, apparently, through unconscious absorption from the air. Our Postmodern moment is permeated with, is defined by, questionings of selfhood and self-reference and narrativity and closure.

When the new fantasy is read together with the new theory, both are enhanced. What we cannot describe we cannot see, and the traditional language of literary criticism offers no words for the temporal disruptions of Diana Wynne Jones or the multivocal narrations of John Crowley. What's going on? asks the traditional critic, confronted by a text in which character, point of view, or conflict, as we thought we knew them in Jane Austen or George Eliot, are barely present. This book tries to identify some of what is going on, to indicate some of the hidden riches in fantasy, making use of insights developed often in response to quite different sorts of narrative. What Genette found in Proust, for example, illuminates fantasy, even as the fantastic text may force an expansion of Genette's theoretical apparatus. Most particularly, theoretical insights that have arisen in response to the narratives of Calvino, Borges, Cortázar, Barth, and Pynchon prove as well to apply to fantasy, even formula fantasy, as I hope will become evident.

I have used the title "Strategies of Fantasy" to try to indicate my multiple purpose. I examine some of the intriguing recent texts to try to determine what strategies of presentation and development allow them to achieve the fantastic. I also point out some strategies available within the fantastic that allow writers to reinvent narrative and all of its components. Finally, I suggest some strategies for reading fantasy, some questions to ask the texts that would not occur to the reader of realistic fiction. Once those questions are asked, I believe, they change our view of all narrative literature, both fantastic and nonfantastic.

Because fantasy has generally been excluded from the canon of great literature—and continues to be excluded despite the demonstrable merits of many of its examples—it can provide a place to stand and judge the canon itself. Readers of fantasy have a certain freedom which is denied to readers within the pale. We may roam at will from adult to children's books, from formula fiction to experimental metafiction, finding pleasure in the most abstruse text and hidden complexity in the most conventional. We may find a continuity in literature that is denied to those who must draw lines and enforce standards. Even though I begin chapter 1 by subdividing the fantastic into what may seem to be hierarchical categories, I wish to assert an overriding kinship among fantastic texts. The mass-market paperback fantasy with a lurid cover is like the limited-edition excursion into fiction by the well-known poet in one all-important respect. Both are outside the culturally defined norm; both are Other.

That otherness makes the fantastic resemble another noncanonical literary category: women's writing. The ability or inability to read fantasy with pleasure divides educated readers nearly as sharply as does gender. Moreover, the deliberate act of "reading as a woman"—which, as Jonathan Culler points out, is an activity that must be learned, within our patriarchal literary tradition, even by women (64)—disrupts some of the same hierarchies of value and conventions of form that the strategies of fantasy deconstruct. What seemed necessary becomes contingent; what was excluded or occluded is brought into view.

The parallel is reinforced by looking at the number of women writers who have found fantasy congenial to their interests as readers and their needs as writers. In chapter 6 I suggest a specific use of fantasy by women writers interested in making the coming-of-age story their own, but the affinity goes beyond any one theme or narrative type. In her acceptance speech for the 1989 Pilgrim Award, Ursula K. Le Guin explicitly makes the connection between the exclusion of women's texts and what she calls the "genrification" of nonrealistic forms like fantasy. "I first thought about this issue of genrification," she says, "not as a woman writer but as a writer of science fiction, fantasy, children's books, and young adult books—four fictional modes categorized by both publishers and academ-

ics as genres, and thereby, by the simple designation, excluded from
serious criticism and consideration as literature." But later, "having been
myself so thoroughly genrified, I was quite ready to accept the feminist
perception of the construction of Literature as essentially political, an
issue of power and control" ("Spike" 18–19).

Le Guin points out that even though *genre* ought to be a neutral
descriptive term, applying to the dominant mode of narrative realism as
well as to such categories as science fiction or mystery, it is applied only to
those genres whose primary readership is outside the power structure of
the academy ("Spike" 19). Many women write in the modes Le Guin lists,
and many of the best are undervalued for that reason. That they find such
genres congenial, nonetheless, is evidence for my argument that nonrealistic literature has something special to offer to the woman writer, who is
already defined by her culture as the irrational, the disruptive, the form-
less, the Other. According to Jonathan Culler, "in recent French writing
'woman' has come to stand for any radical force that subverts the concepts, assumptions, and structures of traditional male discourse" (61). In
this sense, fantastic literature is a woman, a woman who looks, at various
times, like Joanna Russ, like Suzette Haden Elgin, like Sheri S. Tepper,
like Ursula K. Le Guin.

Whether it is seen as threatening or trivial, fantasy is all too often
ignored by serious readers of fiction. Although fantasy has a large and
loyal readership, it lacks the cultural sanction that allows academics to
admit to reading detective novels, another mode that spans the gap
between popular and elite culture. The same readers who devour mysteries by Tony Hillerman and Sara Paretsky scorn to look into books by
equally gifted practitioners of the fantastic, say, Roger Zelazny or Marion
Zimmer Bradley. Thus, many of the readers who are best prepared to
appreciate the more revolutionary strategies of fantasy will never do so,
because they will never open the right books.

While it is not easy to explain the marginalization of fantastic literature on grounds of merit, one can find evidence of the sources of the split
and the ways it has been justified. Since the time of Cervantes, literary
mapmakers have been redrawing the boundaries of narrative. Whereas
once upon a time (I use the phrase advisedly) storytelling was divided into
things that were true—history—and things that weren't—romance—now
the division comes at quite another point. Once the realistic novel was
invented, it claimed kinship to history and denied its ties to romance.
Hence, the gulf opened between histories true or feigned, on the one
hand, and fantasies, on the other. Accordingly, the more history-like a
novel seemed, the more highly it was regarded, and the less incentive
writers had to exploit the romance-like potential of the form.

John Crowley outlines the historical progression in his meta-fantasy *Ægypt* (1987):

> There had been a story in the beginning—in his own childhood and human race's—that a child could inhabit, an account that could be taken literally, about Adamuneve and Christopher Clumbus and a sun with a face and a moon with one too, a stock of stories never discarded but only outgrown, gratefully, name by face, like an old sunsuit. Stories, outgrown just as grownups had always hinted he *would* outgrow them when with fierce literalness he would try to get one or another outlandish detail certified or explained, stories, their aging fabric giving under his fingers. (78)

The outgrown realm of romance never entirely disappeared. Instead, it was relegated, as we have seen, to the margins: to children's books and Saturday matinees and, in rationalized form, to popular storytelling modes like the Western, the detective story, and the formula fantasy. Critical wisdom held that some of these modes were to be dismissed patronizingly, "gratefully," as Crowley says; others should be scorned.

Thus we now have book reviewers and teachers of literature who boast of being unable to read fantasy. They cannot say why: whether it is content or form they object to, magic or reconciliation. They expect all romance to be escapist, all fairy tale to be arch and precious, and those expectations govern their response. They do not realize that these negative qualities are partly the result of the division to which they have acceded, between the real and the un. That division grants significance and substance only to historical and pseudo-historical narratives, leaving the fantastic only a certain airy sweetness, like a meringue.

Yet those who have outgrown romance and rejected fantasy cannot fully understand even their own chosen form, the realistic novel, if they understand only its resemblance to narratives of the real, to history or science. Like the hero of *Ægypt,* they have "got something fearfully wrong" (79). They forget that history is only half of lived reality, and that the other half has somehow to do with mysteries, quests, heroes, comedy, tragedy, impossibilities, symbols, order, and resolution, none of them to be found in the empirical world, the world of historical fact, but always and only in the *stories* by which we make sense of history (Hayden White, *Content* 149).

The fantasies I examine in this book pose particularly interesting questions about the space between history and fiction because they mark off that space in unorthodox and ever-changing ways. Like the European and Latin American masters of the postmodernist metafiction, many contemporary British and American fantasists find popular modes conducive to exploring fundamental principles of signification. They see the story-teller's art as an ancient and worthy one, and entertainment as an essential part of, rather than a hindrance to, serious consideration of the human condition. They are redrawing the map, sallying forth from the mountain fastnesses of fairy kingdoms to recapture territory long lost to the recon-structive imagination.

All of the essays in this volume are attempts, first, to demonstrate how these writers are broadening the range of modern fantasy and, second, to find a theoretical base that can account for their ability to do so. The particular reading strategies I adopt are influenced by the contemporary critical climate. Structuralism, semiotics, reader-response theory, femi-nism, and Bakhtinian dialogism, for example, are the fashionable ways of approaching texts. It may be only an accident of my immersion in the current scholarly conversation that makes me see these as especially revealing of fantasy's enabling mechanisms. Yet because a major result of many of these theories has been an overturning of class- and gender-based canons, they promise to be tremendously liberating to the study of non-canonical fantasy texts. At least these theories provide new contexts and, by doing so, according to the theories, generate new texts as well, trans-forming even such familiar narratives as *The Lord of the Rings.*

The plan of this book reflects my own sense, not only of achievements within the literature of fantasy, but also of the chief misunderstandings of the mode. First, in chapter 1, I attempt to sort out different uses of the term *fantasy,* which is, even within its strictly literary applications, vari-ously applied to a nearly universal impulse, a still-evolving genre, and a strict storytelling formula. Next, focusing on fantasy as genre, chapter 2 looks at a text which forced many readers to recognize that a genre had formed or was in the process of forming out of a group of disparate and eccentric texts. The publication of *The Lord of the Rings* (1954–55), and, even more strongly, the enormous response to its appearance, has been in large measure responsible for separating modern fantasy from its various ancestral forms. Thus, Tolkien's text is a good test case for theories of representation and the fantastic, and, as I hope to show, a test that many theorists fail.

Chapters 3 through 5 deal with the relation of fantasy to literary con-ventions old and new: the traditional narrative building blocks of charac-ter and chronology as well the characteristically postmodern device of metafictionality. In each case, the strategies of the fantasist undermine our sense of the inevitability of conventional modes of narration, thereby reinvigorating the art of narrative.

The last three chapters are all, in different ways, concerned with the relation of text to world. Chapter 6 describes the role that fantastic fiction is playing in women's reinvention of themselves and their place in society and the cosmos. In chapter 7, a hybrid form, science fantasy, shows how the rhetoric and devices of fantasy can be used to reinterpret the narratives that make up science, though we usually think of scientific truths as being somehow more real than the reality we perceive directly. Finally, in chapter 8, I attempt to deal with stories that explicitly challenge the division between reality and imagination, not by saying that fantasy is real but by implying that reality requires something like fantasy to give structure to its otherwise random and inexplicable events.

Many ideas in this book were first worked out in addresses and articles. I am grateful to the following publishers for permission to reprint materials that reappear from earlier versions: Greenwood Press for a version of chapter 3 called "Tolkien, Crowley, and Postmodernism," published in *The Shape of the Fantastic: Selected Essays from the Seventh International Conference on the Fantastic in the Arts,* edited by Olena H. Saciuk (1990); Orion Publishing and Carl Yoke for sections of chapters 4 and 5 derived from "Fantasy's Reconstruction of Narrative Conventions," *Journal of the Fantastic in the Arts* 1:1 (1988); The Kent State University Press for the part of chapter 6 contained in "Women's Coming of Age in Fantasy," *Extrapolation* 28 (Spring 1987); Southern Illinois University Press for a section of chapter 7 that appeared as "Science Fantasy and Myth" in *Intersections: Fantasy and Science Fiction,* edited by George E. Slusser and Eric S. Rabkin (1987); and the Mythopoeic Society (P.O. Box 6707, Altadena, California 91003) and Glen H. GoodKnight for portions of chapter 8, which is an expansion of my guest of honor speech entitled "Reclaiming the Modern World for the Imagination," published in *Mythlore* 56 (Winter 1988).

I also thank those who have read and commented upon parts of the manuscript, including John Kijinski, Colin Manlove, and Seymour Chatman. I found their criticisms helpful in locating flaws, though I have not always followed advice in repairing them. Others have heard me try out ideas at meetings of the Science Fiction Research Association, the Mythopoeic Society, and the International Conference on the Fantastic in the Arts; I wish to thank those groups for their suggestions and their support of the study of fantasy. For support of a different sort, thanks to Jennifer

Eastman Attebery, who underwrote a semester of writing time, and to
Erik Åsard, who had a very flexible notion of my duties as a visiting
lecturer at the Swedish Institute of North American Studies at the University
of Uppsala. Finally, I thank all the fantasists mentioned herein for
giving me much pleasure and for teaching me, as Crowley's *Ægypt* says,

> How history hungers for the shape of myth; how the plots and characters
> of fable and romance come to inhabit real courts and counting-houses
> and cathedrals; how old sciences die, and bequeath their myths and magic
> to their successors; how the heroes of legend pass away, fall asleep, are
> resurrected, and enter ordinary daylit history, persisting as a dream per-
> sists into waking life, altering and transforming it even when the dream
> itself has been forgotten or repressed. (166)

Strategies of Fantasy

ONE

Fantasy as Mode, Genre, Formula

CONSIDER THE FOLLOWING DEFINITIONS:

1. Fantasy is a form of popular escapist literature that combines stock characters and devices—wizards, dragons, magic swords, and the like—into a predictable plot in which the perennially understaffed forces of good triumph over a monolithic evil.

2. Fantasy is a sophisticated mode of storytelling characterized by stylistic playfulness, self-reflexiveness, and a subversive treatment of established orders of society and thought. Arguably the major fictional mode of the late twentieth century, it draws upon contemporary ideas about sign systems and the indeterminacy of meaning and at the same time recaptures the vitality and freedom of nonmimetic traditional forms such as epic, folktale, romance, and myth.

Depending on the examples I choose, I can make an equally strong case for either claim. Fantasy is, indeed, both formula and mode: in one incarnation a mass-produced supplier of wish fulfillment, and in another a praise- and prize-worthy means of investigating the way we use fictions to construct reality itself. It is Italo Calvino and Jorge Luis Borges; it is also Piers Anthony and Robert E. Howard. But a term broad enough to include both *Conan the Barbarian* and *Cosmicomics* threatens to become meaningless. And what about earlier examples: can any definition also accommodate *Alice in Wonderland, A Midsummer Night's Dream, The*

1

Golden Ass, The Odyssey, and perhaps even *Paradise Lost* and *The Divine Comedy?*

However, this breadth belongs only to fantasy-as-mode. Many readers would never think of including Shakespeare or Dante under the heading of fantasy. Instead, they associate the term *fantasy* with a popular storytelling formula that is restricted in scope, recent in origin, and specialized in audience and appeal. They are thinking of fantasy-as-formula, which is essentially a commercial product, with particular authors or publishers' lines serving as brand names for the consumer. As a commercial product, its success depends on consistency and predictability: one expects every box of detergent to be interchangeable with every other. Therefore, the formula end of the fantasy scale is relatively easy to describe, though identifying all of its social functions may be more difficult. The fantastic mode, by contrast, is a vast subject, taking in all literary manifestations of the imagination's ability to soar above the merely possible.

It is difficult to say anything meaningful about either the mode, which is so vast, or the formula, which tends toward triviality. The task would be easier if there were an in-between category, something varied and capable of artistic development and yet limited to a particular period and a discernible structure. I find the concept of genre, as Goldilocks would say, just right. But before I propose ways of defining and studying fantasy as a genre, I must say more about both modes and formulas. The modal approach offers insights necessary for understanding the specific forms—genres or formulas—taken by the fantastic within a particular historical and cultural milieu. Analyzing a formula, on the other hand, can lead to an understanding of the structural basis of a related genre, for though the same grammatical rules may generate both, the formula's structure is more visible, less cloaked in complexities of language and character and theme.

A mode is a way of doing something, in this case, of telling stories. But storytelling is a complicated business. In order to depict the essentials of character, dialogue, action, and physical setting, a writer must find ways not only to present but also to interpret appearance, behavior, thought, and speech. She must base her descriptions on some conception of identity, causality, intentionality, and the benignity, malignity, or indifference of the universe. A mode is thus a stance, a position on the world as well as a means of portraying it.

One of the most famous uses of the term *mode* is Northrop Frye's fivefold division of literature into the mythic, romantic, high mimetic, low mimetic, and ironic modes. These are identifiable according to the status of a story's primary characters: whether they are superior or inferior in degree or kind to their social and physical environment. But Frye sees this scheme, outlined in the *Anatomy of Criticism* (1957), as reflective of a more fundamental division:

> . . . the mimetic tendency itself, the tendency to verisimilitude and accuracy of description, is one of the two poles of literature. At the other pole is something that seems to be connected both with Aristotle's word *mythos* and with the usual meaning of myth. That is, it is a tendency to tell a story which is in origin a story about characters who can do anything, and only gradually becomes attracted toward a tendency to tell a plausible or credible story. Myths of gods merge into legends of heroes; legends of heroes merge into plots of tragedies and comedies; plots of tragedies and comedies merge into plots of more or less realistic fiction. (51)

This underlying polarity is closer to what I mean by *mode* than are Frye's modes themselves. One of these poles has been studied intensively. It is the mode of imitation, in which the aim is to produce the impression of faithfulness to ordinary experience. But the other end of the scale, the counterpoint to mimesis, is not so well established. Frye, in the passage quoted above, has trouble even naming it. It is like myth, he says, but he has already used "mythic." We need another term for the ingredient which, when mixed five parts to one part mimesis, will produce myth; four parts to two for romance; equal portions for the high mimetic; and so on.

This other pole is fantasy. As Kathryn Hume points out, fantasy and mimesis are the fundamental operations of the narrative imagination (xii). They are the more fundamental modes that define Frye's scale of the mythic, the romantic, the ironic, and so on. In fantasy, characters can, as Frye says, do anything: fly, live forever, talk to the animals, metamorphose into cockroaches or gods. In mimesis, by contrast, characters are limited; like everything else in the story they must conform to our sensory experience of the real world. If the world were a simpler place and its rules less ambiguous, we might say that mimesis tells what is and fantasy tells what isn't.

But such a statement takes into account only the surface of reality. The mimesis that results is a superficial, commonsense imitation. Accordingly, even in pursuit of realism, storytellers have repeatedly introduced the fantastic. Though they are contrasting modes, mimesis and fantasy are not opposites. They can and do coexist within any given work; there are no purely mimetic or fantastic works of fiction. Mimesis without fantasy would be nothing but reporting one's perceptions of actual events. Fantasy without mimesis would be a purely artificial invention, without recognizable objects or actions. Even if such a completely fantastic story could be written, no one could read it with any understanding or pleasure. Fantasy depends on mimesis for its effectiveness. We must have some solid ground to stand on, some point of contact, if only with the language in which the story is communicated. Less obviously, mimesis depends on something akin to fantasy for its ability to organize and interpret sensory data, because every organizing schema is the product of imagination rather than simple observation.

Both modes are deeply rooted in ordinary, nonliterary experience. A child's imitation of parental behavior is mimesis. So is telling on a friend, or drawing a tree. Lies, games, and dreams are all fantasy. A writer makes use of these modes, as he makes use of language, to construct an organism, a story, of which the words, sentences, imitations, and imaginings are respectively the atoms, molecules, tissues, and organs.

Within any given work, both modes operate more or less strongly, and with more or less success. Thus, a modal approach to literary texts provides, first, a means of classifying and, second, a basis for evaluation. The realist bias in our critical tradition is such that many commentators confuse these two operations. Erich Auerbach's monumental *Mimesis* (1953), for instance, classifies and evaluates as if there were only one pole, one mode to be identified, one kind of literature worth reading. He gives no indication that a story may be both highly mimetic and bad. The temptation for a fantasy scholar, a temptation which I admit to falling into on occasion, is to reverse the bias, and say, "Don't bother to read such-and-such; it's only a sort of journalism, and not a real story at all. It has no fantasy."

There are several advantages to studying the entire mode of the fantastic. It is broad, so that any findings will have extensive potential application. Because it is a basic operation of narrative, its defining qualities may be arrived at through theoretical speculation, rather than through ad hoc description. It conforms to our ordinary use of the word *fantasy*, which covers a wide range of activities beyond a particular school of storytelling. As indicated above, it offers examples of unimpeachable literariness—Shakespeare, Swift, Dickens, Coleridge—whereas genre and formula fantasy texts are noncanonical by traditional standards. Indeed, most narrative literature, except for an aberrant period from the mid-nineteenth to mid-twentieth centuries (you see the temptation?), has made use of the fantastic. It has, as Hawthorne said, mingled the marvelous in order to heighten contrasts and to bring out the extraordinariness of story, as opposed to the ordinariness of daily life.

But the modal approach does have its disadvantages. Though it promises a theoretical basis, no one seems to agree on what sort of theory to apply. Is the fantastic a function of language, as J. R. R. Tolkien suggests:

based on our ability to separate modifier from substantive and recombine them to produce *green suns* and *flying serpents*? Is it a function of psychology, based on the suppression and subsequent disguising of intolerable realities? Of economics, indicating the misdirection of the revolutionary impulse in the disaffected artist? Of literary evolution, indicating that a worn-out genre is being subverted by its own unacknowledged contradictions? Is it a sort of game? A structure reflecting the brain's own ordering mechanisms? A survival of myth into a rational age?

All of these have been suggested as theoretical bases for the study of fantasy—and some of them, as we will see in the next chapter, as pretexts for condemning either the mode or the genre. Like all literary theories, these are derived from some field of study outside of literature and thus are most convincing when one already accepts the historical or psychological or linguistic assumptions on which they are based.

Any of the theories may be useful in dealing with some branch of the fantastic mode. Some fantasies are intimately connected with language; others are attempts to represent the processes of the psyche. Some reflect social dynamics; others convey an author's or a society's philosophy. Sometimes fantasy is a form of play, while at other times, or even at the same time, it is utterly serious.

Yet the fantastic mode always seems larger than any theory that tries to encompass it. If we say fantasy is a function of language, what about unspoken or unwritten fantasies, as when a caveman draws a stag pierced by his spear or when René Magritte paints a locomotive emerging from the back wall of a fireplace? Both of these are fantastic, in some sense. The former represents one common use of the term *fantasy:* to designate something desired that, though it has not happened, we have no reason to believe could not happen. The latter is more like literary fantasy, in that it portrays a juxtaposition that we perceive as impossible.

These examples indicate that fantasy is to some extent independent of language and may even predate it. Most pictorial fantasy is, however, found in conjunction with verbal narratives. Those that are not explicitly illustrative, like Tenniel's accompaniments to Carroll's *Alice in Wonderland* or Doré's visualizations of Dante, still offer an invitation to the viewer to create a story that will bring about the unachieved or reconcile the impossible. Often the title, like Magritte's *Homesickness* (*Le mal du pays*), encapsulates the implied narrative—not explaining the presence of the winged man and lion on the urban bridge, for Magritte's titles notoriously fail to explain, but providing us with a narrative link. Likewise, representations of the fantastic in dance or mime are nearly always accompanied by verbal texts—if only a printed program—to identify actors and explain events. A danced version of "Sleeping Beauty" relies on our familiarity with written or oral recountings to supply continuity and motivations.

Storytelling itself, of course, usually relies on the properties of language. Language can refer to absent objects, designate different layers of time and represent transitions between them, evoke memories of sensory experience, and provoke emotional reactions. The fantastic strain of storytelling is particularly dependent upon the open-endedness of language: the fact that there are always more sentences available to the native speaker than there are situations to call for them. Thus we can, with even the most elementary vocabulary and grammar, name objects that we have never seen, like Tolkien's green sun. Furthermore, we can narrate events that never happened, and do so in the past tense of historical assertion, rather than in the future tense or subjunctive mood. If we wished to define it linguistically, we might say that the fantastic is the use of the verb forms of reporting for events that in ordinary discourse would require more conditional forms. Rather than saying, "If only I had wings," the fantastic asserts that I do.

But the existence of danced or painted fantasy indicates that the fantastic mode, even when it makes use of language, is also relying on some larger structural organization. Language is a system of arbitrary signs, that is, of sounds or printed shapes, that refer to something else. If, as some linguistic philosophers have claimed, those signs could refer to nothing but other equally arbitrary signs, then fantasy would be impossible, for there would be no choosing between sentences on the basis of their possibility or impossibility. But while individual letters or phonemes are signs in this limited sense, when assembled into words they begin to convey meaning outside of the arbitrary system. It is an arbitrary choice to call a cow a cow and not a lilac, but once that choice is made, I will not be understood if I announce that I am going to go milk the lilacs. At the next level of complexity, the sentence, language can actually begin to resemble its referent, not in its parts but in their articulation. Only at this level can language be said to represent, like a painting, or to move, like a dance.

Out of groupings of sentences, descriptive and narrative, a storyteller generates the larger systems that we call "characters" or "events" or "settings." Unlike the words from which they are made, these stand in relationship to the extraliterary world not as ordinary signs but as what Charles Sanders Peirce called *icons*. By this he meant that the sign is recognizably modeled after its referent—provided we understand the conventions of abstraction at work—in such a way that study and manipulation of the icon can lead to new understanding of the experience to which it relates (Peirce 2:158; ¶ 2.279). One example of an icon is a map of an unknown city, which resembles the city itself sufficiently closely to prevent your getting lost. Even if it is of your own home town, the map may, by virtue of its abstraction from the original, lead you to a new understanding of traffic patterns or the dynamics of neighborhood growth.

To bring this back to the subject of the fantastic, the impossible combinations of object and attribute or agent and action that characterize fantasy *may* refer only to their own self-contradiction. They need not convey any meaning beyond our recognition, based on experience or on cultural indoctrination, that those elements indeed do not belong together: that the sea is not boiling hot, that pigs do not have wings. Yet most writers of fantasy have been drawn to combinations that are more than mere paradox or absurdity. Fantastic literature is full of "loaded" images, concrete emblems of problematic or valuable psychological and social phenomena. The combination of such images into a narrative order is an attempt to achieve iconic representation, so that the narrative can, like the city map, give us new insight into the phenomena it makes reference to.

Sometimes, iconic signs can be modeled on originals that we do not have direct experience or conscious knowledge of. For example, Freud alerted us to the fact that dreams may contain icons of the unconscious mind. For this reason, fantastic literature frequently refers to or imitates dreaming. Dreams, like fantastic stories, often present impossible situations and nonexistent entities that we find mysteriously meaningful. Whatever function we believe dreams serve—wish fulfillment, symbolic confrontation with repressed memories, the unleashing of racial memories, or guidance toward psychic growth—fantastic literature is frequently designed to serve the same ends. The now outmoded convention of a dream framework for fantasy, as in George MacDonald's *Phantastes* or Carroll's Alice books, was probably intended not to undercut the credibility of the stories but to reinforce their ties to the powerful experience of dreaming.

Dream, daydream, hallucination, and visionary states have all provided guidance for writers of fantasy. Michael Clifton argues that the imagery of fantasy reveals its kinship with altered states of consciousness such as hypnosis, meditation, and drug-induced vision (98). Frequently occurring in fantasy are scenes reminiscent of the hypnagogic state, that period of soaring sensations and fleeting visions often experienced just before one falls asleep. Indeed, many fantasy writers describe the composition process as the cultivation of such states, in which the mind generates vivid and unexpected scenes which can then be assembled into narratives. C. S. Lewis, for instance, testifies that "All my seven Narnian books, and my three science fiction books, began with seeing pictures in my head. At first they were not a story, just pictures" ("It All Began with a Picture," *Of Other Worlds* 42).

Thus, even the freest fantasy is in a sense mimetic, for it depicts the associational processes of the unconscious, processes which seem to be most accessible when the rational censor is lulled to sleep and fidelity to surface reality is abandoned.

Some of the iconic signs in fantasy are derived from a single author's dreams or visions. However, the fantastic is not limited to insights into the individual psyche. The first fantastic literature was collective, its symbols shared by entire cultures. The motifs of traditional oral narratives, though probably the product of individual storytellers' imaginations, were selected, altered, and recombined by generations of retellers, each of whom was faced with the necessity of pleasing a live audience. Thus the stories came to represent the desires and perceptions of the group, though the group may not have been consciously aware that it so perceived and desired. Myths, supernatural legends and ballads, magical folktales—all these express a group interaction that is difficult to describe without making analogies to the individual mind. Hence Jung speaks of the collective unconscious, as if humankind shared a single psyche. Fredric Jameson speaks of the political unconscious, and a nation accordingly lies down together on the analyst's couch. The political or collective unconscious may be the product of instinct, or racial memory, or merely of shared experience; it may exist encoded in our brains or may exist only within the texts themselves. It is in any case a powerful force for social cohesiveness and group action, as evidenced by the successful manipulation of mythic narratives by political leaders, evangelists, and advertisers.

Within print-oriented cultures, no mechanism exists for producing such pure expressions of group identity, though the popular media can occasionally produce images that approach the iconic status of traditional myths. However, writers can incorporate structures and motifs from the recorded texts of oral cultures. They can relocate the *Odyssey* in Ireland or in outer space; they can superimpose Odin or Anansi or Coyote on an otherwise mimetically conceived character; they can tell tales of three wishes or three princes or the three realms of the universe. Insofar as the writer can imaginatively recapture the original impulse of a myth, she becomes an honorary member of the tribe from which it emerged.

Nearly all modern fantasy has made such raids on the recorded inventory of traditional narratives. Indeed, some accounts are probably overdrawn, such as Arthurian legend and romance. Reliance on traditional motifs can be an easy way to make sure that the reader will respond to the fantastic. The writer taps the Merlin reflex and watches the reader jump. A few recent fantasies indicate, nonetheless, that not all traditions have been so thoroughly mined, nor have all ways of linking them to the writer's own culture and experience been exhausted.

Realistic fiction is similarly dependent on the devices of past story-tellers, but fantasy is less able to disguise its dependence. It cannot pretend to be unmediated reporting. It cannot be validated by our sense of the realistic, and even though that sense is also determined, to a great extent, by literary convention, we do not perceive the conventions that carve out particular genres and formulas from the mode of realism. If mimesis were not at least partly a matter of convention, there would not be so many rival realisms: social versus psychological, naturalist versus impressionist, stream-of-consciousness versus pseudo-dramatic presentation, minimalist versus the highly circumstantial.

However, the vast, unformed realm of the fantastic is limited not only by convention but also by a desire for iconic significance. The freedom it offers is offset by the need to be understood, and that means channeling the fantastic imagination through the psychological and social codes revealed in individual dreams and in collective mythology. Because the writer desires to connect with the reader, she submits to such restrictions and produces a more or less orderly and comprehensible narrative. She trades away a measure of freedom in exchange for the possibility of meaning.

Some writers seem to be so intimidated by the potential anarchy of the fantastic, so eager for a guaranteed response, that they retreat to the opposite extreme, which results in the predictability of formula. Borrowing from Tolkien and from Disney, they have produced a rigid pattern of setting, character, and plot comparable to the formulas for the detective novel, the Western, and the women's romance. Like these other popular forms, the fantasy formula, sometimes called *swords-and-sorcery,* can be used to generate lively, ingenious, highly entertaining variations on a limited theme. Like them, it represents "a synthesis of cultural symbols, themes, and myths with more universal story archetypes" (Cawelti 33) and hence may be analyzed to reveal widespread cultural values and assumptions.

One appeal of formula fiction is that it can constitute a sort of game or pastime. The skilled author, an Agatha Christie or a Mary Stewart, plays by the rules but finds the loopholes in them. It is not the literariness of a formula story that determines its success but the degree to which it makes the predictable seem fresh and unexpected.

Formula fantasy can be very predictable indeed. It has even spun off a do-it-yourself variation in the fantasy role-playing game. In such games, players follow a sort of recipe for collaboratively "writing" fantasy stories, sometimes through words alone, and sometimes with the aid of props and costumes. The recipe is roughly as follows, for either a game or a book:

> Take a vaguely medieval world. Add a problem, something more or less ecological, and a prophecy for solving it.
> Introduce one villain with no particular characteristics except a nearly all-powerful badness. Give him or her a convenient blind spot.
> Pour in enough mythological creatures and nonhuman races to fill out a number of secondary episodes: fighting a dragon, riding a winged horse, stopping overnight with the elves (who really should organize themselves into a bed-and-breakfast association).
> To the above mixture add one naive and ordinary hero who will prove to be the prophesied savior; give him a comic sidekick and a wise old advisor who can rescue him from time to time and explain the plot.
> Keep stirring until the whole thing congeals.

Yet to say that a book follows a formula is not to say that it is necessarily bad. A poor non-formulaic story may be far worse than a good performance of the formula. Nor is there a clear division between the swords-and-sorcery formula and other uses of the fantastic. Every element of the formula may be present in a tale of sparkling originality. For some writers, narrative constraints seem to act as spurs to the imagination. Like the rules of grammar, such limitations enable invention even while restricting it. The fact that some fantasists do remake the language as they speak it, that they follow conventions but not slavishly, is my primary justification for looking for a middle ground between mode and formula. This middle ground is the genre of fantasy.

The history of the fantasy genre may be viewed as the story of the imposition of one particular set of restrictions on the mode of the fantastic. Modern fantasy begins at the end of the eighteenth century with the first German *Kunstmärchen,* literary imitations of the folktales popularized by Musaeus and the brothers Grimm. Adoption of the mood and setting of the folk *Märchen* was the first such narrowing of possibilities. Each fantasy writer thereafter has reshaped the genre by demonstrating the usefulness of further restrictions. George MacDonald helped to popularize a certain type of hero. William Morris introduced a distinctive vocabulary and style. Lord Dunsany set a fashion in naming places and characters. Tolkien showed that a particular structure worked well. Paradoxically, the more restricted the genre has become, the more productive it is of new texts. As the rules grow more definitive, the game becomes easier for the novice, and, at the same time, more challenging for the expert, the artist who wishes to redefine the game even as she plays it.

The genre poses the continual temptation to accept as formula some prior fantasist's contributions, using them as a shortcut in the painstaking process of inventing a fantasy world. A writer who knows the techniques of the oral narrator thirdhand, not even in the fossilized form of transcribed and edited texts but only as they have been utilized by Tolkien or Lewis or Le Guin, will find it difficult to produce anything *but* formula. The marketplace, too, tends to push fantasy toward formula. Few fantasists are supported by the system of university patronage by which we often recognize "serious" writers. Nor are their books generally published by prestigious hardcover houses and university presses. Instead, distinctive and original novels by Nancy Willard or Paul Hazel appear in identical format and on the same supermarket shelves as the feeblest swords-and-sorcery. Even more problematical, a new writer will often fall somewhere in between these two extremes, producing a first novel that neither remakes the genre nor falls wholly into imitation, and only subsequent efforts reveal whether he will settle for marketable mediocrity or mature as an artist. One of the redeeming features of formula fiction is that it may serve as an apprenticeship for the literary artist: just as Dorothy Sayers could not have written *Gaudy Night* without first working her way through the early Peter Wimsey mysteries, so would Alan Garner have been unlikely to achieve *The Owl Service* (1967) if he had not gained skill and confidence (and an audience) with his apprentice fantasies.

My division of fantasy into formula and genre is therefore a somewhat artificial one. Yet the genre category does seem to be a useful way of designating stories that are more alike than required by the mode, and yet less uniform than dictated by the formula. Some notion of genre is needed to explain just how Garner's mature work differs from his earlier attempts and to show that it is not because both contain dragons that *A Wizard of Earthsea* (1968) bears comparison with *The Lord of the Rings*.

Critics disagree over whether genres should be defined systematically or descriptively, as logical possibilities or as historical facts. Both approaches pose the danger of tempting one to believe too strongly in one's own categories, and so genre criticism is rife with boundary disputes and definition wars. Still, by grouping similar texts together to see how they resemble one another and how far they may diverge without calling for a new category, we can begin to identify the pattern of expectations that allowed them to be written, that their authors drew upon and strained against to produce something unique and yet comprehensible.

The rest of this book is, in a sense, my attempt to define the fantasy genre. I will use the term *fantasy* henceforth for the genre, letting *fantastic* designate the mode: this usage is consistent with a number of critical works on the subject. For instance, modal approaches include Eric

Rabkin's *The Fantastic in Literature* (1976) and Christine Brooke-Rose's *A Rhetoric of the Unreal: Studies in Narrative and Structure, Especially of the Fantastic* (1981), while generic studies include C. N. Manlove's *Modern Fantasy* (1975), Stephen Prickett's *Victorian Fantasy* (1979), John H. Timmerman's *Other Worlds: The Fantasy Genre* (1983), and my own *The Fantasy Tradition in American Literature* (1980).

Nearly every critical text in the field has proposed its own definitions for fantasy and the fantastic. Many of these are grouped conveniently in Gary K. Wolfe's *Critical Terms for Science Fiction and Fantasy* (1986). Virtually all the definitions offered are descriptions after the fact; that is, the critic assembles a body of texts that seem somehow to fit the term and then describes the common feature or features. Literary theorists find this procedure messy, since neither the grouping nor the description is arrived at dialectically. Yet in practice, this method of defining is true to the process of categorization within the human mind.

We often think of genres, like other categories, as territories on a map, with definitional limits marking off hard-boiled from classic detective, or fantasy from science fiction. The critic looks the candidate over, consults his list of characteristics, and assigns the book to the Allied Zone of fantasy or the Soviet Zone of SF, ignoring its ties to cousins on the other side of the wall.

But another model proposed by logicians offers a more flexible means of categorization. Genres may be approached as "fuzzy sets," meaning that they are defined not by boundaries but by a center. As described by George Lakoff and Mark Johnson, fuzzy set theory proposes that a category such as "bird" consists of central, prototypical examples like "robin," surrounded at greater or lesser distance by more problematic instances such as "ostrich," "chicken," "penguin," and even "bat" (122–24). These latter members of the set are described in ordinary language by various hedging terms: they are "technically birds," "birds, loosely speaking," or even "birdlike." A chicken can be a bird to some degree, in some contexts, for some purposes, and be something entirely different, like "farmyard animal," for other purposes. Conversely, an insect may be birdlike enough to warrant a name like "hummingbird moth" or "ladybird"; the name expresses a perceived grouping.

Just so, a book may be a classic murder mystery, like Dorothy Sayers's *Strong Poison,* or more or less a mystery, like her *Gaudy Night,* or somewhat of a mystery, like Mark Twain's *Pudd'nhead Wilson,* or similar to a mystery in some respects, like *Crime and Punishment.* The category has a clear center but boundaries that shade off imperceptibly, so that a book on the fringes may be considered as belonging or not, depending on one's interests. Is *Oedipus* a mystery?

Furthermore, there may be no single quality that links an entire set:

> A beanbag chair may resemble a prototypical chair in a different way than
> a barber chair does. There need be *no fixed core* of properties of pro-
> totypical chairs that are shared by both beanbag and barber chairs. Yet
> they are both chairs because each, in its different way, is sufficiently close
> to the prototype. (Lakoff and Johnson 123)

In dealing with genre, it is our, or at least the writers', perceptions of
category that create the members of the set itself. Hence the importance of
precursors: the stories of Dupin, Holmes, Sam Spade, and Miss Marple
are the "robins" of our fuzzy set of mysteries—or sets, for a viable divergence from type may generate the perception of a new set, as hard-boiled
emerged from classic detective stories.

Is fantasy a fuzzy set? From what center do we perceive it radiating?
Not entirely trusting my own perceptions, I arranged an unscientific
experiment to test them. Calling on acquaintances who have written
scholarship on fantastic literature, I produced a list of forty titles and
asked them to rank those titles on a scale of one to seven. A score of one
described the work as *quintessentially* fantasy; a two said that it is
basically fantasy; three was *technically*; four, *in some respects*; five, the
work is *like* fantasy; six, it is *not really*; and seven, *by no means* fantasy.
Then they were to do the same thing, using the same titles and scale, for
the category "science fiction," a genre with close historical and conventional ties to fantasy.

The titles included novels published as fantasy, as science fiction, and
as (the term is inexact and probably indefinable, but publishers and book
reviewers seem to know what it is) mainstream fiction. Ray Bradbury was
on the list, and so were Aldous Huxley, Joanna Russ, Mark Twain (*A
Connecticut Yankee in King Arthur's Court*), Mary Shelley (*Frankenstein*), Gabriel García Marquez (*One Hundred Years of Solitude*), Bernard Malamud (*The Natural*), Heinlein, Asimov, Lewis, Tolkien, and Le
Guin. My small sampling (14 responses, including my own), my inexact
scale of qualifiers, and my highly idiosyncratic list of titles no doubt
invalidate any results from a statistical perspective, but I did find some
striking patterns.

First, there are, as I expected, no clear boundaries between categories.
Fantasy edges into science fiction; science fiction impinges on mainstream
fiction; mainstream fiction overlaps with fantasy. Second, certain titles
clearly occupy a more central place in people's conception of the genre.
For fantasy, five titles ranked between one and two on average, that is,
were considered to be basically or quintessentially fantasy by my corre-

spondents. The lower the score, the more central. *Dracula* came in with a
1.76; Roger Zelazny's Amber series and E. R. Eddison's *The Worm
Ouroboros* tied at 1.5; *Alice in Wonderland* was even closer to the
quintessential fantasy at 1.42; Le Guin's Earthsea trilogy scored 1.3; and
with a 1.07 representing near unanimity, *The Lord of the Rings* stands in
the bullseye.

So what? I have already admitted that this little exercise has no
scientific validity. However, it does reinforce my own impression that with
the publication and popular acceptance of Tolkien's version of the fantastic, a new coherence was given to the genre. His was not the first
modern fantasy: one might look behind him to the Edwardians—Edith
Nesbit, Kenneth Grahame, and Rudyard Kipling—and before them to the
Victorians—Carroll, Dickens, John Ruskin, Mrs. (Mary L.) Molesworth,
Mrs. (Juliana Horatia) Ewing, William Morris, Charles Kingsley, and
George MacDonald. His may not be the best fantasy: David Lindsay's
might be viewed as more inventive, Mervyn Peake's more vivid, Ursula Le
Guin's more intense, John Crowley's more intricate. But Tolkien is most
typical, not just because of the imaginative scope and commitment with
which he invested his tale but also, and chiefly, because of the immense
popularity that resulted. When *The Lord of the Rings* appeared, we had a
core around which to group a number of storytellers who had hitherto
been simply, as Northrop Frye suggests, "other writers" belonging to no
identified category or tradition (*The Secular Scripture* 42).

Tolkien's form of fantasy, for readers in English, is our mental tem-
plate, and will be until someone else achieves equal recognition with an
alternative conception. One way to characterize the genre of fantasy is the
set of texts that in some way or other resemble *The Lord of the Rings*.

It is possible to be more precise than that. Simply looking at Tolkien's
text itself, one would not be able to guess which of its features have
become dominant in modern fantasy. Do other fantasies echo or anticipate his imagery of stars and jewels, his use of interpolated songs and tales,
his invention of multiple languages, his borrowings from Celtic and
Finnish folklore? None of these turns out to be particularly common
among non-formulaic fantasies. Instead, the works we recognize as fantasy tend to resemble *The Lord of the Rings* in three more fundamental
ways. One of these has to do with content, another with structure, and the
third with reader response.

The essential content is the impossible, or, as I put it in *The Fantasy
Tradition in American Literature*, "some violation of what the author
clearly believes to be natural law" (17). Others define the impossible
slightly differently—Kathryn Hume refers to "departure from consensus

reality" (8), C. N. Manlove mentions the supernatural, Jane Mobley calls it magic—but there is general agreement that some such violation is essential to fantasy. The broader field of the fantastic may include the improbable, the implausible, the highly unlikely, and the as-yet-nonexistent. But fantasy, as it has crystallized around central works like *The Lord of the Rings,* demands a sharper break with reality.

Second, the characteristic structure of fantasy is comic. It begins with a problem and ends with resolution. Death, despair, horror, and betrayal may enter into a fantasy, but they must not be the final word. Much fantasy does not have what we could call a "happy ending." Indeed, the fantasist often seems to start with the idea of such a resolution and then to qualify it, finding every hidden cost in the victory. Le Guin's Ged pays a price in each of the three volumes of her Earthsea trilogy: first his pride, then his self-sufficiency, and finally his powers and nearly his life. Similarly, Frodo is rewarded, at the end of *The Lord of the Rings,* with pain and exile, while Sam faces a diminished world bereft of elven magic. But in each case the problem initially posed by the narrative has been solved, the task successfully completed. If it were otherwise, if, for instance, the Ring were simply hidden again or fallen, despite the heroes' best efforts, into the hands of the Enemy, then we would not have the structural completeness of fantasy, but the truncated story-forms of absurdism or horror.

The structure of *The Lord of the Rings* is that of the traditional fairy tale. It conforms to the morphology described by Vladimir Propp: a round-trip journey to the marvelous, complete with testing of the hero, crossing of a threshold, supernatural assistance, confrontation, flight, and establishment of a new order at home. In a fiction that claimed to be based on life, such invariable resolution might be accused of naiveté, but as a deliberate choice of form in a manifestly unreal setting, it says more about the ways we seek for order than about our expectations of finding it in the real world.

Tolkien himself believed that such an upward movement is inextricably connected with the fantastic; every complete fairy story, he said, that is, every fantasy with an intact structure, must have such a final turn toward deliverance, for which he proposed the term "eucatastrophe" ("On Fairy-Stories" 68). For Tolkien, this term has religious implications, but non-Christian writers such as Le Guin have made effective use of the same structural principle.

This eucatastrophe is essential in producing the effect in the reader that is the third commonly shared property of fantasy. Tolkien calls this effect joy or consolation, but he does not mean by these terms that it is a simple emotional payoff. What the reader experiences in a fantasy is not the same satisfaction that results from getting a Jane Austen heroine married or finding treasure for Jim Hawkins.

A better word might be "wonder." C. N. Manlove makes this a part of his definition for fantasy: "a fiction evoking wonder and containing a substantial and irreducible element of supernatural or impossible worlds, beings or objects with which the mortal characters in the story or the readers become on at least partly familiar terms" (*Modern Fantasy* 1). Manlove rightly connects wonder with the "contemplation of . . . strangeness" (*Modern Fantasy* 7); in other words, it has as much to do with ways of seeing as with emotional response.

The concept of wonder, as a key to fantasy's impact, may best be understood as an alternative formulation of the idea of estrangement. This term has come into English-language critical discourse from two sources: Viktor Shklovsky's *ostranenie*, translated as "defamiliarization," and Bertolt Brecht's *Verfremdung*, which may mean "alienation" (Gary K. Wolfe, *Critical Terms* 31–32). Shklovsky saw estrangement as the essential operation of all literature: through the formal manipulation of their linguistic representatives we are made to see familiar objects and experiences as strange, distant from ourselves. Ultimately, then, literature draws us away from the world we live in—or think we live in, for in Shklovsky and Brecht's Marxist view, the initial familiarity was an illusion produced by the mystifications of bourgeois ideology and hence must be replaced by estrangement as a preliminary step toward social revolution.

Tolkien, a Catholic, also saw the necessity of penetrating illusion. However, for him, such illusion was not politico-economic in origin but was produced by boredom, habit, false sophistication, and loss of faith. The illusion is that the world has become trite or stale. To dispel (or disspell) it, it is necessary to see things in new ways, but rather than making familiar objects seem disconcerting or alien, he thought fantasy could restore them to the vividness with which we first saw them. He called the process "recovery" ("On Fairy-Stories" 57).

In order to recover our sense of something like a tree, it is only necessary to envision a dragon curled around its trunk. Or perhaps merely envisioning is not enough. Tree and dragon must be drawn into a comprehensible pattern, which for human beings means a story. We must know, too, that our fictional representatives will survive their encounter with the dragon and gain new understanding thereby. Tolkien's brand of recovery requires the combination of the familiar and the impossible within the context of an affirming, reordering narrative.

And that is our definition of the genre of fantasy if we take Tolkien as our prototype. It is a form that makes use of both the fantastic mode, to produce the impossibilities, and the mimetic, to reproduce the familiar. The conventions of swords-and-sorcery are not part of the definition: the genre can include stories without hobbits or rings of power or evil magicians. Fantasy does impose many restrictions on the powers of the imagination, but in return it offers the possibility of generating not merely a meaning but an awareness of and a pattern for meaningfulness. This we call wonder.

In the next chapter I will backtrack to uncover some of the theoretical propositions underlying the definitions I have just offered for fantasy and the fantastic. My test case will be, not surprisingly, Tolkien's major fantasy, *The Lord of the Rings;* but I will not be dealing closely with the text itself, which I assume to be familiar to virtually anyone interested enough to have read this far. Instead, I will be looking at the treatment of this prototypical fantasy by representatives of several schools of critical thought. I will be assuming—based on my own and others' reported experience—that Tolkien's story is capable of shifting our perceptions in such a way as to generate wonder, though I do not claim it does so consistently or for all readers. Accordingly, I assert that the task of literary theory is to provide a framework capable of accounting for the story's success on its own terms, rather than denying that its aims are achievable or worth the attempt.

TWO

Is Fantasy Literature?

TOLKIEN AND THE THEORISTS

IN 1968, WHEN NEIL ISAACS AND ROSE ZIMBARDO assembled their first collection of essays on J. R. R. Tolkien, virtually nothing in the way of theory had been proposed for the examination of fantasy. Tolkien himself had made a start, with his essays on Beowulf and on fairy stories, but few looked past his figurative language and religious orientation to see the underlying radicalism of his thoughts on narrative. Accordingly, the critics in *Tolkien and the Critics* (1968) were limited in their discussions of *The Lord of the Rings*. They could describe and quote; make analogies with works in other modes; seek for literary ancestors; pursue themes; evaluate characters and the values they seemed to embody; and discuss stylistic strengths and weaknesses. For the most part they accomplished those tasks with insight and clarity, especially considering the extravagant partisanship of both pro- and anti-Tolkienians at the time. Yet throughout the discussions of these perceptive readers—their ranks included Roger Sale, C. S. Lewis, W. H. Auden, and others less well known but equally astute—one senses that they are struggling to affirm the excellence of Tolkien's text against the weight of a received tradition of critical thought.

The critics were often forced to emphasize elements that conform to standard literary theory, even though those elements may not be characteristic of Tolkien's story as a whole: an ambiguous character here, a manipulation of point of view there, a striking verbal coinage, an allusion, a bit of irony; anything that might compare to the acknowledged values of fiction in the tradition of James or Conrad or Joyce. One is reminded of defenses of Picasso based on the fact that "he really *could* draw when he wanted to."

The most revealing article in the collection is Burton Raffel's "*The Lord of the Rings* as Literature," in which Raffel, who admired the work, was forced to conclude that it was, even so, not literature. It did not fit the criteria he had in mind: style, characterization, and incident. Not just any sort of style, characterization, and incident, for *The Lord of the Rings* (henceforth *LOTR*) certainly has *a* style, does present characters and incidents, but the sort of style that calls attention to its own innovations after the fashion of poetry, the sort of characterization that portrays "significant aspects of human reality" (232), and the sort of incident that seems to occur of its own necessity, rather than according to the dictates of an overall plot. By these standards, *LOTR* is certainly not literature; Tolkien's bumblebee obviously cannot fly. And yet it does fly, as Raffel admits: "Tolkien's three volumes tell an entrancing 'good and evil story' and tell it with power and wisdom; he has succeeded in constructing a self-contained world of extraordinary reality—and grace" (218). Despite all this, "making stories, even wonderful stories, is not the same as making literature" (219).

Raffel is convincing. We must either redefine literature or exclude Tolkien—and with him much of modern fantasy. If it is true (as I believe) that all the closely observed characters and finely tuned prose in the world won't make a dull story readable, and that to judge from the relative rates of success and failure in existing fiction, spinning wonderful stories is the rarest and most difficult of literary skills, then we need a new definition of narrative literature, and such a theory must be able to account for the felicities as well as the obvious failings of a work like *LOTR*.

Any theory of narrative that could explain what is going on in Tolkien's epic would also force a reexamination of other stories, both fantastic and nonfantastic. Common assumptions about how narrative is organized, what its building blocks are, and how it relates to the world of extraliterary experience all prove inadequate to explain fantasy, insofar as *LOTR* typifies the genre. Even so, if we can begin to explain how fantasy operates, we may find that other kinds of fiction operate in some of the same ways, but on a level usually concealed by surface circumstantiality.

In the last two decades, narrative technique, formerly taken at face value or neglected in favor of fiction's dramatic and stylistic elements, has finally come under systematic scrutiny within the Anglo-American critical community. There seem to be two main reasons for this shift of attention toward narrative. One is the increasing availability of English translations of pioneering explorations by Russian and French scholars such as

Vladimir Propp, Viktor Shklovsky, Mikhail Bakhtin, Claude Lévi-Strauss, Gérard Genette, Roland Barthes, and Tzvetan Todorov, all of whom share an interest in the ways narrative is structured and how those structures carry significance. The belated discovery of this group, whose writings in their own languages actually span several decades, produced such excitement as to overshadow, for a time, efforts made by theorists writing in English, such as Northrop Frye and Wayne Booth.

The other reason for a new interest in narrative organization was the appearance of a new kind of narrative which violated conventional narrative codes. Generalizations about what literature is and does, which may have been adequate to explain everything from Jane Austen to William Faulkner, broke down when it came to Borges's "Pierre Menard, Author of the *Quixote*" (1962) or Calvino's *The Castle of Crossed Destinies* (1977).

And so a host of new theoretical terms gained currency as tools for analyzing the new fiction and unearthing hidden patterns within the old. Many, perhaps most, of the postmodernist texts that had called for new terms of analysis were fantastic, and so, not surprisingly, scholars have begun applying contemporary theory both to the mode of the fantastic and to the genre of fantasy, even to Tolkien's genre-crystallizing tale. Thus we come to the central question behind this chapter: how has *The Lord of the Rings* fared in the hands of theorists, and what have they had to say that was not covered by earlier critics?

Few of the Continental theory-builders have looked directly at the genre of fantasy. Propp worked with the traditional fairy tale, a primary source for the modern fantasy tradition, and so his "morphology" is a tremendously useful mode of analysis for fantasy, but Propp himself does not trace the borrowing of the fairy tale pattern by literary artists. Todorov has confused matters greatly in *The Fantastic* (1975), which has almost no bearing on the kind of fantasy we are discussing here—a product of diverging meanings for the word *fantastic* in French and English. "La litterature fantastique" is an entirely different genre, confined almost exclusively to the nineteenth century and represented in English by such texts as Henry James's "The Turn of the Screw."

Direct application of contemporary theory to *LOTR* has been largely the work of second-generation theorists. One example is Rosemary Jackson, in *Fantasy: The Literature of Subversion* (1981). Jackson comes to fantasy formidably armed with theoretical weapons, primarily Freudianism, Marxism, and structuralism, not in their original, blunt-instrument forms but as revised and refined by Jacques Lacan, Julia Kristeva, Louis Althusser, Fredric Jameson, Jonathan Culler, and other major contemporary proponents. Starting from this base, Jackson proposes, first, that fantasy is fundamentally a literature of desire and, second, that its ventures into the nonexistent are really ways of challenging the existing political, social, and economic order. These two propositions are more closely connected than it might appear. According to Jackson, desire is not a simple psychological drive, but the tension produced by the social inhibition of such drives: "a lack resulting from cultural constraints" (3). Hence, a literature of desire is of necessity a literature, as her subtitle indicates, of subversion. When fantasy describes the impossible, Jackson says, it is really manifesting the forbidden.

Jackson's theory is compelling and proves fruitful in analyzing texts ranging from Kafka's "Metamorphosis" to Carroll's *Alice in Wonderland*. The trouble is, when she gets to the Tolkienian expression of the fantastic, she attempts to use her theory as a standard. The function of fantasy is to express desire in a subversive guise, she says, but Tolkien's fantasy attempts to do something else. Rather than broadening her theory to fit the exception, she concludes that *The Lord of the Rings* is a failed fantasy, and along with it the works of Kingsley, MacDonald, Le Guin, and Lewis. Her comments on the genre converge curiously with those who condemn it from the perspective of mimetic theory: it evades reality. The reality she is speaking of is interior, rather than exterior, but the tone of her accusation is the same:

> The moral and religious allegories, parables and fables informing the stories of Kingsley and Tolkien move away from the unsettling implications which are found at the centre of the purely "fantastic." Their original impulse may be similar, but they move from it into religious longing and nostalgia. Thus they defuse potentially disturbing, antisocial drives and retreat from any profound confrontation with existential dis-ease [*sic*]. (9)

Not only does Tolkien's fiction represent a retreat, but the justification of his own practice he offered in "On Fairy-Stories" is "transcendentalist" and, accordingly, "sentimental," "nostalgic," the product of "an outworn liberal humanism" (153, 155).

In looking at the story of *LOTR*, Jackson focuses on Tolkien's portrayal of social systems and finds that, despite his obvious dislike for twentieth-century industrial society, he can be faulted for "supporting a ruling ideology" (155). In other words, instead of criticizing the noise, pollution, dehumanization, destructiveness, and sheer ugliness of modern cities, which may be found in any social system, he should be attacking only those ills specific to capitalism.

Jackson fails to make use of the theoretical tools at hand to offer any real insight into *LOTR*. She mentions that Tolkien sets up an aesthetic standard for morality—"virtue lies with a beautiful Elvish Speech, evil with an ugly Black Speech" (156)— but fails to note that this equation is a rhetorical device to alert the reader to the presence of evil, not an attempt to define evil linguistically. She objects to Tolkien's Medievalism on the grounds that he is evading the writer's responsibility to represent his own age, forgetting that she has elsewhere claimed (rightly) that every text inevitably represents its own age. Tolkien's Medieval world is not the historical Middle Ages any more than Pierre Menard's *Quixote* is Cervantes's. Jackson faults Tolkien's use of such fairy tale elements as the impersonal narrator and the happy ending because they allow the reader to be passive: "The reader, like the protagonist, is merely a receiver of events which enact a preconceived pattern" (33). Yet Tolkien's story surely requires as much active collaboration from the reader as any experimental novel, for it asks our continuous assent to what we know to be impossible, thereby altering the status of every assertion within the narrative.

The instances of fantastic narrative Jackson praises are subversive because they confound our expectations. "They assert that what they are telling us is real—relying upon all the conventions of realistic fiction to do so—and then they proceed to break that assumption of realism by introducing what—within those terms—is manifestly unreal" (34) Yet Tolkienian fantasy may be equally subversive, for it asserts that what it is telling us is unreal and then proceeds to break that assumption of unreality by drawing upon the conventions of realistic fiction. Why should the one technique be praiseworthy and the other subject to condemnation?

The answer seems to be either that Jackson is not applying theories with equal justice or that the theories themselves are inadequate to explain what is going on. Like the theories of language that reduced speech to a matter of simple stimulus and response—and held sway for decades because they allowed no evidence other than the sort of observation that confirmed their assumptions—these theories of narrative tend to reduce all texts to a few simple patterns, and those texts least amenable to such reduction are ranked lowest by the theoreticians.

Yet even an uncongenial theory may bring insight if it is applied with sympathy. Jackson's characterization of fantasy as a literature of desire is suggestive. Desire of all sorts is a key ingredient in *LOTR*: hunger, thirst, religious longing, greed for power, death wishes; desires fulfilled and unfulfilled, acknowledged and repressed. But Jackson offers only two operations that a narrative can perform with desires. It can either express or expel them. Thus, disturbing elements can overwhelm the narrative, in good or "radical" fantasies, or be thrust out of it, in bad or "sentimental" ones.

In both cases, the desires are considered to be preexisting, the product of the clash between psyche and society. According to C. S. Lewis, however, fantasy illustrates a third operation that can be performed on desires: arousing them. A fantastic tale stirs longings that either did not exist previously or that the reader was not aware of: "It stirs and troubles him (to his life-long enrichment) with the dim sense of something beyond his reach and, far from dulling or emptying the actual world, gives it a new dimension of depth" ("On Three Ways of Writing for Children," *Of Other Worlds* 30).

Lewis's language here, like Tolkien's in "On Fairy-Stories," reflects his religious orientation; however, this statement cannot be dismissed as "transcendental." For Tolkien and Lewis, it is true, longing for the nonexistent could be a preliminary to personal experience of the divine. Yet Lewis's formulation can be translated into purely materialistic terms and still remain valid. These new desires are most probably built from existing elements. Just as complex emotions like love are built from less lofty impulses, for example, the pairing instinct and the sexual drive, the *Sehnsucht* or longing engendered by fantasy has its roots in the various physical and emotional hungers we have all experienced from infancy. The dream of paradise is not a mere displacement of nostalgia for the womb, as Jackson suggests; however, it may develop from such an emotion by adding to it and restructuring it. Whatever its origins, such longing is an important component in the cognitive shift toward wonder engendered by successful fantasy.

Jackson's lack of sympathy with Tolkien and his ilk prevents her from seeing continuities between their fantasy and the work of the fantasists she admires, just as it causes her to undervalue Tolkien's and Lewis's speculations on the nature of fantasy. She even goes so far as to cite the politically more correct W. H. Auden as a source for Tolkien's ideas: "W. H. Auden's *Secondary Worlds* influenced Tolkien's formulation of secondary, autonomous, imagined realms in *Tree and Leaf*" (182). The Auden essay she cites appeared in 1968; Tolkien's "On Fairy- Stories" appeared as a lecture in 1938 and in print in 1947.

Christine Brooke-Rose's *A Rhetoric of the Unreal* (1981) adopts many of the same theoretical methodologies as Jackson's study, but it is not so obviously partisan and so manages to find more of the pattern and purpose in Tolkien's work. Brooke-Rose, herself a novelist in the self-reflexive fantastic manner, is interested in how the system of language is able to sustain secondary systems within it. These are the conventional rhetorics by which we seek to represent the world of experience and give it order and significance.

A narrative rhetoric is a way of presenting information about characters, setting, events, and so on, so as to determine the parameters of the reader's response. A particular rhetorical choice will cause some elements within the story to be suppressed, others emphasized or even "overdetermined" through redundancy and other devices. Time sequence, for instance, may be indicated once by verb tense, again by adverbial markers, and yet again by characters commenting on it. Generally, overdetermination of one element of a narrative is balanced by withholding of information in other areas. For example, Brooke-Rose points out that although Irving's "Rip Van Winkle" belabors the fact of its time paradox—twenty years spent in a single night—it leaves symbolic implications almost entirely for the reader to supply from bare hints. Thus, she concludes,

> it is clear that over-determination in one area does not alter our feeling of something else being there, less immediately accessible, which gives the story its charm and quality (to use evaluative words), or (to avoid them) its underlying structure and coherence. (112)

Another kind of rhetoric may overdetermine symbolic applications of the text while leaving other dimensions, such as physical environment, purposely vague.

Brooke-Rose's theory allows us to view the spectrum of narrative possibilities, from sober pseudo-history to fantastic adventures, as a choice of rule-bound activities, rather like meaningful games. Choose one game and your rules are set, by precedent and by expediency: some gambits demonstrably work better than others. Nevertheless, within a given rhetorical pattern, original discourse is possible. Rules may even be bent or borrowed from some other pattern. Most importantly, though Brooke-Rose does not say so, this theory implies that no one rhetoric is inherently preferable, though one story may be more successful than another.

The rhetorics Brooke-Rose identifies include those of the realistic novel, science fiction, the folktale and its literary imitations, the playful text, and the ambiguous tale (Todorov's "fantastic"). These categories converge and their various rhetorical systems likewise exhibit overlapping features. Realism shares with science fiction its insistence on a "megastory"—a field of historical, geographic, or scientific information— against the backdrop of which the plot is enacted (86). In science fiction, of course, much of this megastory is invented by the storyteller and must be supplied surreptitiously as the story unfolds.

The folktale and the ambiguous tale both present carefully interlocking actions, each the explanation for the next, but in the folktale everything fits together in the end, while in the ambiguous story we are left with two or more mutually contradictory patterns, like puzzle pieces that can fit together to make a triangle, a circle, and a star, but with a gap somewhere in each design.

Brooke-Rose devotes a full chapter to *The Lord of the Rings*. The primary rhetoric here is that of the marvelous, for which she essentially adapts Propp's morphology of the fairy tale. A tale of the marvelous proceeds by unfolding a series of structural elements, which Propp called "functions"—characters like the hero, the helper, and the opponent, or incidents like interdiction, crossing of the threshold, gaining of treasure, and return. Often these functions are doubled or tripled, a rhetorical device that emphasizes their status as parts of a pattern, a story, rather than mimetic renderings of real human beings and lives. The pattern they make is usually a quest.

LOTR adopts the rhetoric of the marvelous in many respects, except that the quest is inverted: the adventurers seek to lose, rather than acquire, a valuable object. It also differs from most traditional uses of the marvelous in the degree of reduplication of functions. Instead of one helper or "adjuvant," there are eight, counting only those actually traveling with the hero. Several of these break off temporarily to serve as secondary heroes in subsidiary quests.

Brooke-Rose gets impatient with Tolkien, finding the plot unnecessarily embroidered with secondary characters and false climaxes, but she has no theoretical basis for her complaint. Tolkien is certainly following the rhetorical rules of his chosen narrative form, albeit to an unprecedented degree. At most we can say that he has overdetermined the structural basis of the story.

Another of Brooke-Rose's objections to Tolkien's handling of the marvelous is his use of *a posteriori* justification for the action. Why does Boromir attempt to wrest the ring from Frodo? In a traditional fairy tale we might not ask; it just happens that way. But Tolkien provides some possible answers—Boromir's clouded heritage as the descendant of not-quite-kings, his city's desperate need, his father's growing despair, his proud and hasty temperament. Brooke-Rose finds these explanations unconvincing. The real reason for Boromir's actions, she says, is that the plot demands them:

> his function is wholly to introduce dissension in the Company . . . , *so that* it can split, *so that* Frodo and Sam should be alone in the quest, *so that* the adventures may be separated. When that is achieved Boromir is got rid of (dies). (237; emphases in text)

Any psychological justification for these actions is secondary to the narrative necessity that calls them forth.

Organization by *so that* is another kind of overdetermination. It too is a feature of traditional fairy tales. Why does Cinderella's mother die? So that her father can marry again, so that Cinderella may be mistreated by stepmother and stepsisters, so that her fairy godmother may intervene, and so on. Tolkien certainly does not attempt to conceal this rhetorical element. He even has characters whose primary function seems to be pointing out *so thats*. Brooke-Rose refers to Gandalf as "the great explainer" (237), and Elrond, Aragorn, Faramir, and others play the same role on occasion. Though she does not follow up on the idea, her observation could lead to insight into the sources of Tolkien's skill, for he evidently recognizes as part of the tale's meaning the very fact that it is a constructed thing, and not a found object.

Why does Brooke-Rose object to Tolkien's use of the rhetoric of the marvelous in a tale of the marvelous? Because she is applying standards based on other rhetorical modes. Inadequately motivated action is a lapse, not in fantasy, but in the realistic novel, where we expect to be provided with enough character analysis to conceal the mechanical nature of the plot. Brooke-Rose objects to *LOTR* because it offers some of the features of realistic fiction, but not to the same degree we have come to expect. Boromir is assigned motives of pride and envy, but those motives are, in comparison with the psychologizing of a Henry James, transparent and static. In this mix of modes, "the obviousness belongs to the marvelous, the insistence to realism" (249).

And that is Brooke-Rose's great analytical insight, which is also her primary failing when she translates analysis into judgment. *LOTR* does mix modes. Its sense of vastness, of stories behind stories, of characters who enter the story without being profoundly affected by it, who disappear into untold stories of their own; these impressions derive from Tolkien's adaptation of the rhetoric of the real, rather than the unreal. At the same time, Tolkien makes use of fairy tale inevitability and of role-defined characters, like the many elves who seem to exist solely to "send messages, offer rest, cure, magical gifts, solemn welcomes, farewells and counsels . . ." (250).

In Brooke-Rose's view the mixture represents "the weakest feature of both the realistic and the marvelous combined . . ." (250). She finds that "the techniques of realism, when invading the marvelous, have a very curious effect. For they not only weigh down and flatten out the narrative like an iron, they actually change its genre, or come very near to doing so" (254). Again filtering out the negative evaluation, which is a matter of taste masquerading as analysis, we may borrow Brooke-Rose's conclusion to help explain why *LOTR* remade the genre of fantasy.

If we accept her description of Tolkien's technique without agreeing that such a technique is necessarily problematic, we can see that the rhetoric of the realistic-marvelous can produce effects not available to either of the parent modes. It is, for instance, the probable source of

LOTR's curious resistance to allegorical readings, including that which Brooke-Rose tries to impose (254). Frodo, Saruman, the Ring remain stubbornly themselves—suggestive of, but not reducible to, components of twentieth-century life. Tolkien's overdetermined rhetoric will not allow us to bypass the concrete instance and proceed directly to the moral application.

Like Jackson, Brooke-Rose is unwilling to follow up the implications of her own methodology when it comes to Tolkien. Both writers seem incapable of paying close attention to the text, as shown by remarkable carelessness with detail. In *A Rhetoric of the Unreal*, Brooke-Rose turns Sam Gamgee's name into the Hindu-sounding "Gamjee" (237), misspells the name of the dwarf Balin as "Belin" (244), states that "Gandalf, though a wizard, can only perform minor magic" (245), and refers to Arwen's "brother Elrond" (252). Names and magic are important and related parts of the megatext of *LOTR*. These lapses suggest that she does not see the way Tolkien has structured the story so that megatext is as important as foreground narrative. His rhetorical strategy directs us to look for significance in the interrelationships of the two rather than either alone.

These two examples of theoretical approaches to Tolkien indicate that the chosen theories are not being applied rigorously. There may also, however, be limitations in the theories themselves. The dominant literary theories from early Modernism to late Structuralism have rested on a triple base: Saussure, Marx, and Freud. These three giants of the late nineteenth and early twentieth centuries attempted to treat human studies from a scientific perspective—Saussure applying to language, Marx to history, and Freud to psychology the methods of the natural sciences. By imitating the objective stance and descriptive technique of physics or biology, they hoped to clear away centuries of circular reasoning and unnecessary assumptions. Hence their importance to literary theorists who wish to be equally scientific.

But large areas of human experience do not lend themselves to exploration through the methods of the physical or even the biological sciences. The German philosopher Wilhelm Dilthey offers a cogent critique of attempts to model human sciences after natural ones. He insisted that we cannot ignore the evidence of internal awareness, nor can we equate a lived experience with the sense perceptions from which it springs. Predictive models, too, falsify human experience by imposing a deterministic form of causation, omitting awareness and choice from the course of events (Makkreel 66). Trying to be scientific, Saussure reduced language to an arbitrary self-referential pattern, Freud viewed the psyche exclusively in terms of its infantile origins, and Marx accounted for all historical events as manifestations of the struggle for means of production. Once liberating truths, these formulations have all too often hardened into sets of blinders, preventing the wearer from seeing the whole scope of human affairs.

But there are alternative theories. Some of these have been applied to Tolkien with results that demonstrate their ability to illuminate areas of experience left untouched by orthodoxly scientific theory.

In place of Saussurean structural linguistics, which focuses only on the abstract language system (*langue*) as it exists in a single point in time (synchronically), T. A. Shippey has applied Tolkien's own discipline of philology to his created world, looking at language as it changes through time (diachronically) and as it appears in the specific utterances of individuals (*paroles*). Though one risks loss of perspective in taking Tolkien at his own valuation, by doing so, Shippey has produced what is unquestionably the most knowledgeable and suggestive reading of *LOTR* and its supporting texts, such as *The Silmarillion* (1977) and *The Hobbit* (1937).

Shippey's thesis in *The Road to Middle-Earth* is that Tolkien created the megastory of Middle-earth and large parts of the foreground narrative out of his understanding of the evolution of languages, primarily English and its Germanic cousins. The nineteenth-century philologist viewed language not as some abstract structure, a code that refers only to other codes, but as a treasury of words, each of which carries its history along with it. Modern linguistics, which has made great strides in formulating the laws governing syntax and discourse, is far less successful in explaining the workings of the lexicon, the body of knowledge that links abstract grammatical structures to audible sounds and sounds to meanings. Tolkien's philology has more in common with contemporary semiotic studies, with its concern for the signs and their interpretation, than with structural linguistics, which more or less ignored words.

For the lover of words, or philologist, every word is a window into the past. A word like *elf* is also *aelf* and *ylf* and unrecorded but reconstructible forms in proto-Germanic and Indo-European; it is a part of *elfshot* (both the tiny projectile points given the name in England and the diseases they were thought to cause) and of Alfred (elf-counsel); it is *Beowulf*, which speaks of *ylfe* as children of Cain, and *Sir Gawain and the Green Knight*, which calls the green giant an *aluisch mon* or elvish man, and the ballad of "True Thomas," who meets "the queen of fair Elfland" (Shippey 45). The word is, in fact, the sum of all its forms and meanings and uses over time, insofar as those are recoverable through philological research.

Language records a culture's habits and concerns, its physical environment and its myths. Just as we can reconstruct prior forms of words, producing the hypothetical spellings marked by asterisks in the etymological section of a dictionary entry, we can reconstruct the worldview of those who used those words, producing what Shippey calls an "asterisk reality" (15). Tolkien's Middle-earth is—to an extent most critics are unaware of—such an asterisk reality, an attempt to make the world perceived by the listeners of *Beowulf* accessible to readers in the twentieth century. If this world is an invented one reflecting the cultural assumptions of its inventor, so are all such archeological reconstructions. Tolkien's is an archeological, rather than historical, enterprise: he is seeking the city buried beneath the modern city, the language which our language rests upon and conceals.

It is possible to miss the theoretical implications of Shippey's detailed exploration of Tolkien's names, invented languages, and storytelling techniques. It may seem to be merely another sort of close reading or source analysis. Yet Shippey's illumination of Tolkien's techniques forces a reconsideration of such critical dogmas as the "death of the author." Does language generate texts, using the living author as a sort of involuntary medium? Surprisingly, Tolkien's example might lead us to a qualified "yes." It could well be said that the English language wrote *LOTR*, but with J. R. R. Tolkien as active collaborator. Without his erudition and his imaginative understanding of the connotative and contextual, as well as structural, properties of language, the text could not have come into being.

In much the same way that the Saussurean view of language can prevent our seeing what Tolkien was doing with language in *LOTR*, a strictly Freudian reading of the text obscures, rather than illuminates, much of its psychological basis. Freudian psychology—or rather a popularized form of Freudianism, which is what I am really talking about here—can offer certain insights into the symbolic subtext of *LOTR*. It does not take much stretching to see the id popping out in Tolkien's underground horrors: the many dark tunnels, the swarming orcs and trolls, the long-suppressed fiery Balrog and the gross and devouring Shelob. In Shelob and other spider figures we would not be far amiss in seeing the dark side of the mother figure: Tolkien's unacknowledged resentment of his own mother's untimely death. The same maternal image in its positive form is Galadriel—who is, like Shelob, powerful, female, and a spinner.

It takes more ingenuity to find an Oedipal conflict, but no doubt a determined Freudian could do so, perhaps in Frodo's acquiring of the female-symbol ring from the weakened father figure, Bilbo. But such armchair psychologizing leads us astray if we conclude that this is the major role played by Bilbo. We have learned little about the dynamics of the story.

Freudian analysis of the text is most productive in examining those parts of *LOTR* that are most like horror fantasy, the Lovecraftian touches that Tolkien uses for contrast with his idylls and elvish reveries. Freud's psychology seems particularly attuned to the rhetoric of horror, which is all about the revelation of suppressed secrets and disgust for bodily functions. All horrific fantasy, from *The Monk* to Stephen King, may be viewed as variations on a primal scene. It is regressive and disintegrative, breaking the psyche down to its component drives. The Freudian notion of art, as something to be worked through, used up, and left behind once it has brought to consciousness whatever complex it was encapsulating, may explain the process of reading or writing horror fiction, but it is of little use in illuminating fantasy.

The brand of psychology that mirrors the rhetoric of fantasy is Jung's. Whereas Freud looks to origins, Jung looks to ends: not where we came from but what we may grow into. Freud looked back to tragic myths, like those of Oedipus and Electra, for insight into the unconscious mind; Jung looked at fairy tales. *LOTR* can be accommodated to the Freudian model only as Cinderella's stepsister fit into the glass slipper, with much distortion and more omission, but it wears the Jungian schema like a running-shoe. Gandalf is a textbook example of the Wise Old Man archetype; Frodo and his companions, especially the shadow-Frodo Gollum, represent the fragmented psyche on the road to selfhood. It is so simple as to make one uneasy; can an enterprise so obvious reveal anything of value?

It can, if we do not push it too far. Jungian analysis shows us what is already apparent about a fairy tale or a fantasy, because those forms are inverted relative to the realistic fiction. What is deep structure in a Dickens novel is integument in a fantasy. Fantasy starts with a symbolic narrative: it must present archetypes and it must, if it follows the comic, fairy tale morphology, move toward self-integration. But if a fantasy is to be successful, those abstract universals must be recreated afresh from the author's individual experience and self-knowledge. Hidden within Gandalf the Wise Old Man, the archetypal guide and protector, is a realistically depicted, irascible old tutor—undoubtedly a blend of characters met by Tolkien in real life, including himself in the role of educator—which represents the way Tolkien had personally experienced the function of that archetype.

What a psychological reading of fantasy should aim for is not merely identifying complexes or archetypes, depending on the particular metaphoric scheme on which the psychology is based. Rather, it should see how the narrative makes use of these mechanisms for self-analysis, which is what all such systems really amount to. They are not real entities within the brain but ways of coming to understand and make use of that organ's manifold electrical and chemical operations. Freud's ego, id, and superego; Jung's archetypes: these also are narrative functions— characters, as it were—within fantastic narratives that help us comprehend our own perceptions and motives. Jung's narrative of the maturing self is the more nearly parallel to Tolkienian fantasy and therefore the more useful in exploring it.

An exemplary instance of the method is Patrick Grant's "Tolkien: Archetype and Word" (1981), which does not oversimplify Jung's conception as I have done above and which points out the limits of any such superimposition of systems. Grant implies that every fantasy is a descriptive psychology as well, so that what is really needed is a Tolkienian reading of Tolkien. By serving as a point of comparison, Jung may help us arrive at such a reading; so, to a lesser extent, may Freud; so might the fantasy writer who is their equal in formulating narratives about the psyche, George MacDonald.

The Lord of the Rings is about language and about inner experience, but it is also about the exterior world of affairs. Therefore we need a third theoretical model for analyzing fantasy's treatment of social action and interaction, and the currently dominant model in literary studies is based on Marx's dialectical analysis of history.

We have already seen, in Jackson's study, how a Marxist perspective may be used to dismiss Tolkien. Fredric Jameson, a much subtler practitioner of Marxian or Althusserian reading, similarly avoids close examination of *LOTR*: in the otherwise compelling study "Magical Narratives: Romance as Genre" (1975), he shunts attention away from the primary contemporary form of the magical narrative by labeling it "archaic nostalgia" (161). One wishes he, or someone of his persuasion but more in tune with Tolkien's text, would investigate the problem of what he calls "the ideological nature of *form*" (161) as it is raised by fantasy. Much could be done with his insight that "as a literary device, this vision of a realm of magic superimposed on the earthly, purely social world, clearly outlives the particular historical and ideological contradiction [of the emergence of class rivalries within feudalism] which it was invented to resolve, thereby furnishing material for other quite different symbolic uses as the form itself is adapted to the varying historical situations . . ." (161). But perhaps the assumptions of Marxist and even Jamesonian neo-Marxist thought preclude the necessary willingness to accept Tolkien's categories.

For the external world examined by *LOTR* is not fundamentally the economic and political one which Marxism posits. Politics in Middle-earth is primarily symbolic (Tolkien is not talking about reviving the divine right of kings when he installs Aragorn as High King), and the improbability of its economic system is an indication of its creator's lack of interest in such matters. But that is not to say Tolkien is silent on the problems of the human community.

Marxism posits history as the primary science and economics its irreducible base. Within its human universe, rival groups strive for control of means of production, triggering social evolution as antithetical forces generate a new synthesis. But means of production in the truest sense are not part of the social world at all. Factories do not produce; they alter natural products to meet human needs. The human household (to take *economics* back to its root word *oikos*) is inescapably dependent on the greater and elder *oikos* of nature, and an economic interpretation of human interactions is necessarily secondary, whether we recognize it or not, to an ecological one.

One attempt at an ecological reading of fantasy is Don D. Elgin's *The Comedy of the Fantastic* (1985). Elgin borrows Joseph Meeker's thesis that comedy, which emphasizes reconciliation, regeneration, and human foibles and limitations, generates a perspective more conducive to the survival of our species than the view of man as tragic hero, above and apart from the world of nature. Fantasy, which maintains a comic vision despite the preference of philosophers and literary critics for tragic nobility, represents a kind of realism in that it accepts our place in a larger system and also in that it insists on the primacy of immediate experience over abstraction, even such abstractions as *humanity, nature, good,* and *evil.*

That last point may seem to be contradicted by *LOTR*. Isn't the whole story about the conflict between good and evil? Jameson suggests that the magical narrative is shaped by ethical judgments which are abstracted from social distinctions:

> it is becoming increasingly clear that the concept of evil is at one with the category of Otherness itself: evil characterizes whatever is radically different from me, whatever by virtue of precisely that difference seems to constitute a very real and urgent threat to my existence. So from earliest times, the stranger from another tribe, the "barbarian" who speaks an incomprehensible language and follows "outlandish" customs, or, in our own day the avenger of accumulated resentments from some oppressed class, or else that alien being—Jew or Communist—behind whose apparently human features an intelligence of a malignant and preternatural superiority is thought to lurk—these are some of the figures in which the fundamental identity of the representative of Evil and the Other are visible. The point, however, is not that in such figures the Other is feared because he is evil; rather, he is evil *because* he is Other, alien, different, strange, unclean, and unfamiliar. (140)

It is true that Tolkien makes use of this tribal mentality, incorporating longstanding English prejudices to portray evil beings as short, swarthy Easterners speaking harsh (i.e., Slavic-sounding) languages. But it is also true that this ethical division is rendered increasingly invalid as the story progresses, as evil emerges among the kingly Gondorians, the blond Riders of Rohan, the seemingly incorruptible wizards, and even the thoroughly English hobbit-folk of the Shire. Rather than abstracting good and evil, Tolkien localizes such qualities in specific actions: on the one hand, Sam's sharing of the burden of the Ring; on the other, Denethor's attempt to burn his living son Faramir along with himself.

The Ring itself may seem to be an abstraction, and many readers have tried to fit it into an allegorical system, but it resists such a reading because it is not really abstract. It is a concrete object with physical properties like color, weight, an inscription that shows up under heat, and an extraordinarily high melting point. It also possesses specific magical capabilities which are the sources of its power to corrupt. Don Elgin provides a more satisfactory analysis of the role of the Ring than do any of those critics who try to equate it with pure evil. Tolkien conceives of the Ring as a tool with one function: mastery. Its possessor can exert his will over the lesser rings of power, as its inscription indicates, and over other beings and even over nature. Such mastery isolates (hence the Ring's power to make its wearer disappear) even as it aggrandizes. Elgin points out that the same taint affects even those characters we take to be the embodiment of good: the bearers of elvish rings Elrond, Galadriel, and Gandalf. Though these three are diametrically opposed to Sauron, they are also akin to him, and *LOTR* is the story of their fall as well as Sauron's. In the end, they must pass away from the earth because "the noble, heroic, tragic age has passed . . ." (58). Tolkien portrays this passing with regret, but he ends his story with the comic affirmation represented by Sam and his family.

To Elgin, this affirmation is neither nostalgic nor transcendental. Tolkien draws on the ancient magical worldview and the comic narrative structure because they offer something to the present. He is not merely indulging in pastoral idealization of nature; rather, he is imagining new ways of integrating human life into the systems of nature, as represented by Tom Bombadil's refusal of ownership over the land (39–40) or Treebeard's stewardship of the forest (40–42). In generating narrative embodiments of an ecological viewpoint, myth provides more valid models than does history, for history tends to divorce humanity from the natural world, while myth continually reminds us of our place within it. But the myths must be remade, for they contain also the seeds of the alienating, abstracting perspective that turns the stranger into the Other and the earth into a commodity.

By juxtaposing philology with linguistics, archetypes with Oedipal conflicts, and ecology with economic determinism, we see that a text like

LOTR offers new perspective on literary theory itself. Theories like Marxist historicism, which do nothing with this text except proclaim its deficiencies, are shown thereby to be less universal than their practitioners are wont to claim. Other theoretical approaches prove their utility by enriching our experience of the text and by building bridges between it and other aspects of our lives.

The three theories I have offered as alternatives to the "scientific" approaches of Saussure, Freud, and Marx are not the only alternatives. I selected them because they are as at least as scientific as the theories they oppose; because they are fundamentally in harmony with Tolkien's practice and his own narrative theory, as expressed in the essay "On Fairy-Stories"; and because all three make certain claims about literature that might help us revise canonic assumptions such as those of Burton Raffel, cited at the beginning of this chapter.

First, they point out that the revival of "archaic" narrative forms and motifs—fairy tales and myths—is not necessarily a nostalgic enterprise. Insofar as those myths continue to reside in our language and to offer insight into our psychic organization and our relationship to nature, they are not archaic but contemporary. They reflect human nature as it is perceivable in our time and place, though that may not be the same human nature they reflected in Homer's day. All three theories emphasize the role of storymaking in our efforts to invent integrated selves and a comprehensible world.

Second, they challenge the notion that literature is essentially, or even primarily, representational. They speak of words and names, of archetypal figures, and of narrative movement—sheer storytelling—as the fundamental stuff of literary art. Mimesis enters in later, as part of the process of developing and differentiating a particular narrative from its structural siblings. Fantastic invention serves the same differentiating function, with equal validity.

Third, they all see the narrative sequence as a system, rather than as a neutral structure. The latter may be viewed as a mere vehicle for carrying more important elements like character-portrayal or societal analysis. The former is its own justification; it exemplifies the system-building by which we conceive of reality. A comic narrative like *LOTR* is a model of an affirmative, integrative worldview, which is not necessarily naive, escapist, or reactionary.

In short, we have not one but three theoretical bases for understanding the development of the genre of fantasy as it was described in the preceding chapter. Fantasy's reliance on the impossible, its comic structure, and the resulting positive estrangement or wonder it can offer the reader can all be understood as resulting from a particular use of language, a technique for investigating the workings of the mind, and the adoption of an ecological treatment of humankind's place in the natural world.

I do not believe this is a full account yet of the inner dynamics of *The Lord of the Rings,* let alone all of modern fantasy. For instance, very little has been said about the social and political backgrounds of the writing of the text. The Marxist critics are too concerned with blanket condemnations of European capitalism to make any of the finer distinctions necessary to place Tolkien in his true setting, using the biographical data assiduously gathered by Humphrey Carpenter, and others have shown little interest.

Likewise, any claims about the story's psychological validity or linguistic comprehensiveness should be tested against a feminist analysis: *LOTR* is a thoroughly man-centered work and offers a considerable challenge to a woman reader who wishes to share in its affirmation, though many women readers have found the effort worthwhile.

Some sort of rethinking of the nature of narrative is necessary if we are to read Tolkien without warping his text into a deviant or even failed example of a conventional novel. The various theoretical systems outlined above put us in a better position than that of the critics of 1968 to appreciate or question Tolkien's narrative tactics. But these theories must be applied impartially and with full attention to the text, or they will reveal less than do the unsystematic intuitions of careful and sympathetic readers.

Above all, it must not be assumed that Tolkien was unaware of the things he was doing, that he achieved all his effects by accident or deviated from novelistic conventions without knowing the alternatives. On the contrary, Tolkien and other writers of fantasy have been, if anything, more conscious of the fundamental operations of narrative than are the critics who accept as absolutes such concepts as plot, character, point of view, and the separation of text and world. In the next chapters I will be looking at some of the more subversive formulations of these narrative conventions by Tolkien and his successors within the modern fantasy tradition. Along the way I will continue to draw upon a range of fashionable and forgotten theories in order to bring to the foreground fantasy's capacity to challenge our notions of literary art.

THREE

Fantasy and Postmodernism

SOME OF THE THEORISTS discussed in the previous chapter were not really interested in the genre of fantasy at all. They turned to Tolkien only because he could not be avoided in discussing twentieth-century uses of the fantastic. What they really wanted to talk about was the fantastic of Kafka, Robbe-Grillet, Pynchon, Barth, Calvino, Borges, and Lem. There is no question that these writers have created a lively genre within the fantastic mode. Following Lance Olsen, we can identify this genre with a general cultural movement, usually called Postmodernism because it seems a deliberate reaction against most of the central tenets of Modernism.

There are many versions of Postmodernism, just as there are many manifestations of the Modernist impulse. What we call Modernism is not quite the same thing in dance as in architecture, in sculpture as in music, for each of these arts has its own formal properties and its own traditions to rebel against. Even within literature, Modernism is one thing if we define it through the practice of T. S. Eliot and quite another if we select Gertrude Stein. It follows that a writer who wishes to be Postmodern, to revise or supplant Modernism, will create one sort of Postmodernism if he starts from Ernest Hemingway, and a drastically different one if he starts from Virginia Woolf.

Yet there are some persistent tendencies within Modernism, and these lead to equally consistent trends within its would-be successor. Most

Modernism seeks to penetrate falsehood, flout convention, and recreate a more authentic self (Singal 14). Therefore Postmodernism deliberately perpetrates illusions, adopts and even exaggerates outmoded conventions, and attempts to de-center the individual. Whereas Modernism values density of expression even unto unintelligibility, Postmodernism conceals sophistication within ingenuous simplicity, borrowing the styles of comic books (*Cosmicomics*) and primers (*Ragtime*). Modernism is often elitist or "Mandarin"; Postmodernism, especially in its Latin American manifestation, populist. Modernism, with some exceptions, prefers the stark, the spare, the somber; Postmodernism inclines toward the extravagant, the colorful, the patently impossible.

The Postmodern fantastic is widely recognized as a formidable new force in the literary world. It is a powerful current sweeping into the mainstream. Admirers of its dazzling metafictional play and freewheeling inventiveness rarely acknowledge, however, that these characteristics are shared with what has long been considered a minor literary backeddy, namely the genre we have been calling fantasy.

Modernism and Postmodernism encourage quite different reading strategies, each designed to valorize the dominant texts of its own cultural moment. Yet a Modernist reading is unlikely to lead to understanding or appreciation of fantasy, even a fantasy produced during the heyday of Modernism, whereas a Postmodernist reading of fantasy can illuminate both recent and older works.

I propose to examine fantasy, first, as it appeared to readers with Modernist expectations, and then juxtaposed with examples of the Postmodern fantastic. Two texts are particularly well suited to this exercise by reason of their respective positions in literary history. One is, once again, *The Lord of the Rings*. The other is John Crowley's 1981 novel *Little, Big,* in which the fantasy tradition descending from MacDonald, Morris, Tolkien, and Lewis converges with Postmodern uses of the fantastic.

Literary histories written from a Modernist perspective simply omit fantasists like Tolkien, Lewis, and E. R. Eddison. Their works are too different from the dominant texts of the period. Only in the bold experiments of Pound, Eliot, Stein, and Joyce, such historians imply, did such psychic bombshells as Freudian psychology, Einsteinian physics, world wars, the Russian Revolution, industrialization, deracination, and a general loss of faith find adequate literary expression.

This viewpoint is reinforced by analogous events in other arts. Along with Modernism's disruption of narrative sequence and characterization, we have the Modernist impulse in music stretching melody and harmony to their limits and beyond; in painting taking leave of perspective and then of representation altogether; in architecture stripping away ornamentation—that is, texture and color and form not demanded by the structural requirements of the building itself. Works of genius like *Ulysses, The Rite of Spring,* and the Bauhaus Building helped define the age.

And, in so doing, they pushed many works out of the critical spotlight. It was possible to dismiss even a popular composer like Ralph Vaughan Williams as an epigone, a living fossil, because he stuck to traditional forms and motifs, to melody and tonality. Similarly, architects like Julia Morgan do not even appear in architectural histories intent on tracing the triumph of the International Style over moribund classicism. Morgan's mentor Bernard Maybeck, whose inventive, theatrical designs are the opposite of Bauhaus starkness, was "for most of his life . . . considered an eccentric in appearance, demeanor and practice—an engaging architect but hardly an important one" (Longstreth 128).

For strikingly congruent reasons, J. R. R. Tolkien incurred the scorn of critics like Edmund Wilson, who did not see how one could seriously read a tale with "no serious temptations," a lack of "development in the episodes," characters who "do not impose themselves" as personalities, and "no instinct for literary form" ("Orcs" 329). This was not a kind of literature for adults in the twentieth century: it had no complexity of the right kind and was too elaborate in the wrong ways.

Wilson's model for Modernism is scientific realism fused with the surrealistic language of the French Symbolists, and indeed most Modernist novels seem to be essentially mimetic reporting striving to turn into lyric poetry. Tolkien aims at neither of those goals and instead concentrates on action and scene within an obviously arranged plot. Wilson's preference for a particular brand of Modernism shows in his praise of Yeats for outgrowing the "self-consciously archaic" fantasies of his early poetry (*Axel* 44). By contrast, he entertained no doubt that Dickens's work was seriously weakened by the fact that "he has admitted a larger conventional element than the greatest novelists ordinarily allow and has been content to press into service melodramatic 'good' characters and villains into whom he has scarcely projected himself at all" (*Axel* 177). Hence it is no wonder he dismisses Tolkien so easily, since Tolkien's archaism is more deeply engrained than Yeats's, and his fiction is more thoroughly melodramatic (if by melodrama we mean the portrayal of good and evil characters) than even Dickens's.

What makes Vaughan Williams, in music, and Tolkien and Lewis, in fiction, seem such "dinosaurs" (Lewis, "De Descriptione Temporum" 14) is not merely their use of unfashionable conventions and folk motifs. A respectable Modern like Bartok used symphonic conventions and folk tunes; Eliot wrote poetry that rhymed and scanned; Faulkner incorporated Southern folktales into his fiction—but they all did so with irony, distorting even as they borrowed. Vaughan Williams's fantasias and Tolkien's fantasies are non-ironic, and therefore, apparently, inartistic.

The course of twentieth-century literature can be viewed as the gradual spread of irony into every phase of storytelling. Writers turned an ironical eye on mores, then on character and motivation, on documentary realism, on the arrangement of incidents into a plot, on chronological narrative, and finally on language itself. Each had fallen under suspicion as a means of discovering and conveying meaning. "Ironic" became a term of the highest praise to Modernist critics like Cleanth Brooks. To tell a story, as Tolkien seemed to do, as if it were still possible to take heroes and happy endings seriously was to incur the disdain of the apostles of Modernism.

Tolkien committed such sins as telling his story from beginning to end; dividing his characters into good and evil; allowing the good to triumph over the evil; writing in transparent, workmanlike prose instead of densely poetic language (even in his verse); resting comfortably within a tradition rather than Oedipally slaying his ancestors; and supposing the fairy tale might be a suitable form for adult reading. His work showed virtually none of the signs of excellence that critics like Wilson looked for, and they were unprepared to see the sorts of excellence he had achieved.

In the 1950s, when *The Lord of the Rings* finally appeared in print (its elements having been gestating for most of Tolkien's adult life), it seemed that Modernist irony and Tolkien's fairy tales could have nothing in common; how, then, have the literary descendants of the twain begun to meet?

John Barth has described the *reductio ad absurdum* of the Modernist movement in his essay "The Literature of Exhaustion" (1967): "Somebody-or-other's unbound, unpaginated, randomly assembled novel in a box" (29). According to Barth, Modernism's program of "disjunction, simultaneity, irrationalism, anti-illusionism, self-reflexiveness, medium-as-message, political olympianism, and a moral pluralism approaching moral entropy" ("Replenishment" 70) was accomplished by the middle of this century. Readers had been educated, had grown wary of literary illusion, could no longer take narrative or narrator for granted. Nothing remained for Modernist writers to exercise their irony upon, and so Modernist fiction had nothing more to say.

After nothing, however, must come something again. When all the conventions have been destroyed, says Barth, "it might be conceivable to rediscover validly the artifices of language and literature—such far-out notions as grammar, punctuation . . . even characterization! Even plot!— if one goes about it the right way, aware of what one's predecessors have been up to" ("Exhaustion" 31).

In a follow-up essay called "The Literature of Replenishment" (1980), Barth listed writers he considered Postmodernist, hailing the "synthesis of straightforwardness and artifice, realism and magic and myth" (71) in works by Italo Calvino and Gabriel García Marquez. He praises these works for being every bit as self-aware and carefully wrought as Modernist fictions and yet joyous, fertile, and (to Barth at least) accessible. Calvino's *Cosmicomics* (1968), for example, is readable on many levels, from the simplest to the most sophisticated, because it manages to keep "one foot always in the narrative past—characteristically the Italian narrative past of Boccaccio, Marco Polo, or Italian fairy tales—and one foot in, one might say, the Parisian structuralist present; one foot in fantasy, one in objective reality" (70).

So it seems the Postmodernist prospectus, both an extension of and a corrective to Modernism, involves a return to early narrative forms—the fairy tale movements and mythic structures that never really disappeared from more popular forms of literature—but with an awareness of their artificiality. Postmodernism is a return to storytelling in the belief that we can be sure of nothing but story. The result is not the alienation of Modernist fiction or the obscurity of its Mandarins but rather, according to Alan Wilde, a "radical vision of multiplicity, randomness, contingency, and even absurdity" (10). Wilde calls this vision a new "horizon of assent" because it has, by abandoning the last forlorn hope of order, enabled writers to take pleasure in indeterminacy, coincidence, and the storyteller's traditional freedom of invention.

Though Postmodernism is still fundamentally skeptical about humankind's ability to portray any kind of reality through literature, though it is still highly self-reflexive or metafictional, its metafictions are by no means narrow, self-consuming, or nihilistic. Rather, they are characterized, according to Patricia Waugh, by

> a celebration of the power of the creative imagination together with an uncertainty about the validity of its representations; an extreme self-consciousness about language, literary form and the act of writing fictions; a pervasive insecurity about the relationship of fiction to reality; a parodic, playful, excessive or deceptively naive style of writing. . . . In providing a critique of their own methods of construction, such writings not only examine the fundamental structures of narrative fiction, they also explore the possible fictionality of the world outside the literary fictional text. (2)

It should be clear to attentive readers of *The Lord of the Rings* that Postmodernist criteria are much better suited to explaining its success than are realist or Modernist criteria. Tolkien's trilogy is playful, fantastic, and tied to the narrative past, especially to myth and its near relatives, legend and fairy tale. In addition, it is as reflective of linguistic theory as any truly Postmodernist novel. As noted in the last chapter, T. A. Shippey's *The Road to Middle-Earth*, taking as its central thesis Tolkien's statement that "the 'stories' were made rather to provide a world for the languages than the reverse," reveals that *The Lord of the Rings* is in large part a study of the way language shapes cultures and individual perceptions (19).

Like Postmodernist fiction, Tolkien's work is always metafictional, most explicitly in his shorter fictions "Smith of Wootton Major" and "Leaf by Niggle," but also in the longer tales. Niggle's painted leaf, which grows by degrees into a tree and then an entire world, is Tolkien's illustration of the process by which order and significance are created out of seeming accident and inconsequentiality. In "Smith of Wootton Major," the artists are what we might dismiss as artisans—a cook and a black-smith—but Tolkien finds their tradition-bound crafts, like that of the storyteller, capable of enchantment. In *The Hobbit* and *The Lord of the Rings,* we find frequent stories within stories; references to plans and prophecies; artist figures like Gandalf (first seen as an artificer of fire-works); and metaphors like the road that goes ever on, taking the unwary traveler from his own doorstep into realms of fable. Such devices are ways for Tolkien to comment on the storytelling process.

Whether expressed through metafiction or through the direct dis-course of his essays, Tolkien's view of literature is that handling an inherited form is as difficult and as rewarding as breaking new ground, particularly when that inherited form has been in eclipse. He was par-ticularly interested in the intricate mechanisms that give shape to nar-rative, a form of artistry he thought undervalued since Chaucer's time. Beginning in the Renaissance, he felt, literary criticism had essentially concerned itself with dramatic rather than narrative artistry. In his con-cern for the latter, he is closer to the Postmodernists than to the critics of his own day, who, he says, are "likely to prefer characters . . . to things" and to "misunderstand pure story-making, and to constrain it to the limitations of stage-plays" ("On Fairy-Stories" 51).

However, despite his interest in language, metafiction, and the origins of narrative, Tolkien is not a Postmodernist. For one thing, he was born at the wrong time. Just younger than T. S. Eliot, just older than Hemingway, he was in the very middle of the Modernist generation and, like other writers of his time, was shaped by war and disillusionment. *The Lord of the Rings,* with its troops and trenches, its heroism and despair, its beleaguered home front and its enemy to the East, is as much a product of World War I as is *The Sun Also Rises.* Also like his contemporaries,

Tolkien was schooled in commonsense realism and had to find his own way around it. A Postmodernist would not say, as Tolkien does, that "creative Fantasy is founded upon the hard recognition that things are so in the world as it appears under the sun; on a recognition of fact but not a slavery to it" (55). Hard recognitions and grim reality are characteristic of Modernist fiction, of *Dubliners* and *In Our Time,* and though Modernist critics might condemn Tolkien for wishing to escape from objective fact, they would agree with him that it exists.

Postmodernists, on the other hand, are fond of blurring the distinction between fiction and truth, pointing out that no text is a mirror of reality and that even history is first and forever a form of storytelling. Hence, though both Tolkien and Postmodernists are interested in literary frames, like the fairy tale's "once upon a time" or the mock-scholarly introduction, Tolkien differs from Borges or Lem in that he avoids the characteristically Postmodernist violation of that frame. He is interested in sustaining illusion, not violating it.

Additionally, Tolkien, unlike most Postmodernists, does not juxtapose contemporary culture and traditional storytelling forms. He draws from folk culture but not from popular art or literature (although, of course, his creations have since entered into pop culture, usually in simplified form). By avoiding contemporary references, he finds it easier to sustain what he calls "secondary belief" in both the magical world and the action within it (37).

Writers stimulated by the example of Tolkien have generally followed him in producing distanced, quasi-medieval fantasy worlds. However, it is possible to work within the fantasy tradition and yet play freely with narrative frame in the Postmodernist manner, causing the self-contained fantasy world to intersect with contemporary life. John Crowley, one of the best of post-Tolkienian fantasists, has managed to do just that in his science fantasy *Engine Summer* (1980) and in his American fairy tale *Little, Big* (1981).

The latter novel is long and dense with allusion and incident; a complete inventory of its riches would take considerably longer than this chapter. The book combines the mythic pattern of prohibitions, magical helpers, quests, and comings of age with a sharp and humorous delineation of American artifacts, language, landscape, and values.

The story spans seven generations of a single family, shifting from the recent past back to the 1890s and ahead to some time in the future, perhaps to the end of this century. The primary settings are an unnamed city that is obviously New York and a country estate named Edgewood somewhere upstate.

The house at Edgewood was built by the founder of the family, John

Drinkwater, of the Beaux Arts architectural firm of Mouse, Drinkwater, and Stone (reminiscent of McKim, Mead, and White). Drinkwater himself is a conflation of several nineteenth century figures with confusingly similar names. Like Andrew Jackson Downing, he is the author of a book called *The Architecture of Country Houses*. Like Alexander Jackson Davis, he is known for borrowings from "the Greek, Gothic, French, Italian Renaissance, Egyptian, and even Oriental schools" and is "credited with having inspired many queerly designed houses of the Victorian era" (*National Cyclopedia* 22: 174–75). And, like Andrew Jackson Davis, he is a spiritualist, obsessed with the possibility of communion with the Other World.

Drinkwater's house reflects both his interests. Intended to serve as a sampler of Drinkwater's eclectic Victorian repertoire, it has five fronts, each in a different style, with fictive details to make each facade seem to be a whole building:

> . . . as they passed, it seemed to fold like scenery; what had looked flat became out-thrust; what stuck out folded in; pillars turned pilasters and disappeared. Like one of those ripply pictures children play with, where a face turns from grim to grin as you move it, the back front altered, and when they reached the opposite wall and turned to look back, the house had become cheerful and mock-Tudor, with deep curling eaves and clustered chimneys like comic hats. (30–31)

This house of illusions is believable as an example of Victorian extravaganza, but it is also a work of fantastic art. Hence it functions as a stand-in within the story for the story itself, with transformations, sudden reverses, and internal complexities. Thus, perhaps because it is a story made three-dimensional, the house acts as a door to the other world, through which the impossible can invade the world of everyday.

The primary narrative line of *Little, Big* deals with the marriage of Smoky Barnable and Alice Dale Drinkwater (nicknamed Daily Alice), the architect's great-granddaughter. The opening scene, in which Smoky walks out of the city through thinning suburbs and industrial parks to the true countryside around Edgewood, is a classic fairy tale threshold crossing. It is also a metafictional device leading the reader from one mode of reading, the realistic, to another, the fantastic. Arriving at Edgewood for his wedding, Smoky enters the complex plot that has long been weaving around the Drinkwater family. Important strands in this plot concern John Drinkwater's courtship of Alice's great-grandmother, the Don Juanish career and subsequent metamorphosis of her grandfather, the substitution of a changeling for her sister Sophie's child, Alice and Smoky's son Auberon's adventures in the city (which include a thwarted love affair, a job writing a television serial, and a lapse into dereliction), and the return of Frederick Barbarossa from the cave in Germany where, according to legend, he has been sleeping for eight centuries.

All of these subplots are tied together because they are the working out of a plan conceived by supernatural beings, evidently the fairies. These beings, powerful and unpredictable like the local spirits of European folklore, are not named by the characters or narrator, just as English fairies are referred to only by such euphemisms as "the Good People" to avoid calling their attention to oneself. Alice and her family simply speak of "them." "They," it seems, have chosen the Drinkwaters and their kin to replace them as a new fairy pantheon, while they go on to some higher order of existence.

Crowley tells his tale in a variety of styles, some parodic, others straightforward, frequently adopting the leisurely voice and expansive vocabulary of a nineteenth-century narrator. The old-fashioned quality serves as another framing device, establishing the narrative as something other than faithful reporting of everyday life. It is underscored by the book's design, with ornamental chapter headings, chapter titles, subheads in the margin surrounded by flourishes, and architectural-looking designs to mark chapter ends (only in the original trade paperback; much of this effect is lost in the ugly mass-market edition). These devices contribute to the book's humor and frequently add an overlay of irony to the narrative while allowing Crowley to maintain the illusion of sincerity and un-self-consciousness in the narrative voice, as if he were telling of the perfectly ordinary doings of ordinary people.

Crowley may have learned from Tolkien how to use the rhetoric of realistic fiction to present the marvelous. He certainly follows Tolkien's example in persuading us to accept impossibilities by tying them to familiar objects. Alice's wood-paneled station wagon, Smoky's borrowed wedding suit, and cousin George Mouse's inexhaustible stash of recreational drugs anchor the magical narrative in a recognizable world, just as Bill the pony, Sam's cooking gear, and Barliman Butterbur's good beer help counterweight the marvels encountered in *The Lord of the Rings*.

Another Tolkienian method of validation is to refer to literary or folk tradition as witness to the plausibility of the events described. Whereas Tolkien generally alludes to medieval cosmology or rural English legend, Crowley turns to the unacknowledged sources of the middle-class American worldview, such as superstitions, children's books, and popular culture. Early in the novel, for instance, Alice goes to the pond to consult with Grandfather Trout—who is both a real trout and her real grandfather, formerly known as August Drinkwater. We accept the impossible situation because Crowley presents it in the context of familiar elements.

These come from folk belief (Alice brings the trout out of hiding by clapping rocks together under water), from advertising (Alice poses over the pool like the girl on the White Rock soda bottle), from Thornton Burgess's Mother West Wind stories, from the Mock Turtle scene in *Alice in Wonderland,* and from Walter de la Mare's "The Listeners" (1912) (" 'Tell them I came, anyway,' she shouted after him, her voice small against the waterfall's. 'Tell them I did my part,' " 18). One is left with an impression not of impossibility but of inevitability, of familiar fragments assembled into the order they were meant to have.

In the face of such circumstantiality, readers must go back and reinterpret statements we originally took for metaphor: "The stream that hurtled ceaselessly through the cleft to plunge into the pool made a speech as it did so, a speech repetitive yet always full of interest; Daily Alice listened, though she had heard it all before" (17). Abstraction gives way to the concrete and literal, and the long-lost freshness of an expression like "babbling brook" is recovered through the estranging process of fantasy.

But Crowley knows that this effect is best produced by copying Tolkien's sobriety in reporting marvels. Whatever else is mocked or placed in doubt, the supernatural is played straight, as Tolkien says it must be: "since the fairy-story deals with 'marvels,' it cannot tolerate any frame or machinery suggesting that the whole story in which they occur is a figment or illusion" ("On Fairy-Stories" 14).

Here, I believe, is where Crowley's work is more satisfying than the Postmodernist narratives that undercut marvels with such devices as a sudden shift in tone, as if to say, "We're all adults here and we don't *really* believe a horse can fly." Crowley, knowing full well we do not believe, reports the impossible so faithfully that we begin to question the nature of belief itself.

In several of Crowley's fictions, he demonstrates the ability of seemingly naive forms like fantasy and science fiction to examine complex relationships of narrator and narrative or story and belief. Sometimes, however, the sophistication of his inquiry is not evident until one compares one of his stories with the more obviously metafictional fables of a Postmodernist writer like John Barth. If one reads Crowley's novel *Engine Summer,* for example, alongside the "Bellerophoniad" section of John Barth's *Chimera* (1972), one becomes aware that both writers are working with similar materials, but that Crowley's novel is the subtler treatment. Both stories turn on the idea of a narrator actually becoming the story he tells. Barth credits this transformation to the workings of the Greek gods, an Ovidian metamorphosis, but because his narrator has already proven unreliable and because of authorial intrusion and anachronism, the reader is not invited to explore the implications of the change. It is all too plainly nothing but a literary device, an allegorical fantasia on semiotic theory.

Crowley rationalizes his transformation through a science-fictional device. It is gradually revealed that the narrator whose story we have been reading, who is called Rush that Speaks, exists in the narrative present only as a set of memories recorded on crystal. These memories must be temporarily assumed by another person in order to recapture the experiences of the original actor. By keeping the reader's attention on the concrete reality of this device within the text, rather than letting it evaporate into metaphor, Crowley is able to explore subtler distinctions between memory and truth, history and storytelling. For instance, the story varies according to the temperament and interests of the volunteer who assumes Rush that Speaks's identity; a listener comments to the temporary Rush that "I don't think any other loved Once a Day [Rush's lost love] as much as you, I mean as much as in this story. And I never heard of the fly caught in plastic before" (173). Barth's method allows for no such distinctions.

In *Little, Big,* as in *Engine Summer,* Crowley is interested in making fantasy comment on the way we use fiction to understand the world outside the story, and he finds he can do so most effectively by turning his irony everywhere except on the illusion itself. Since fantasy makes no attempt to hide its fictionality, it takes no effort at all to puncture the bubble but considerable artifice to maintain it. Crowley has learned from Tolkien that breaking a frame is not the only way to call attention to it.

Though Crowley has been reluctant to say very much about his own writing, it is evident that he is aware of contemporary metafictional practice and intentionally departing from it. The testimony of his fiction is supported by his comments on Alasdair Gray's *Lanark* (1985), in the review for the *New York Times Book Review,* "From Unthank to Glasgow and Back" (1985). He describes Gray's indulgence in frame breaking: "An epilogue placed well before the end takes the form of a dispute between Lanark and a character—not named Alasdair Gray— who says he is the author of the novel. The two argue about how the story should end and we are given an elaborate lecture on the novel's pla-giarisms and antecedents, complete with footnotes" (15). But Crowley goes on to comment that "this sort of self-reflexive set piece will one day seem as corny and as redolent of this period as deathbed scenes of Victorian novels seem now" (15). He recognizes that the form of fantasy itself implies a degree of self-reflexiveness and authorial manipulation of reality. It makes its metafictional statements most effectively when it seems most ingenuous, as in Tolkien's perfectly sincere, perfectly impossi-ble narrative.

However, Crowley differs from Tolkien in two ways. One, as mentioned above, is his incorporation of contemporary life into fantasy. *Little, Big* makes use of the fantastic, as *The Lord of the Rings* does, to estrange and thereby renew our vision of simple and timeless things: rocks, trees, bread, moonlight, and song. Yet he also uses it to comment on popular media, conspiracy theories of history, the rise and fall of the automobile, urban ethnicity, 1960s druglore, fashions in spiritualism, and political demagoguery.

The other difference is in the manner in which Crowley uses metafictional elements. Whereas Tolkien upholds a fast distinction between what he called primary creation (the world we live in) and secondary (the world of story), and his metafictional devices serve chiefly to establish the importance of storytelling in its own secondary sphere, Crowley indicates that there is no primary creation in that sense, or that it is approachable only through the imagination.

Hence his characters are aware that their lives are part of a Tale, that any order or purpose is determined by "them," the magical beings who are thus stand-ins for the author.

Different characters have different perspectives on the Tale. Alice takes it for granted; after informing Smoky that their meeting was foretold,

> "But see?" she said. "It was all meant to be. And I knew it."
> "But why," he said, delighted, in torment; "why are you so sure?"
> "Because it's a Tale. And Tales work out."
> "But I don't know it's a tale."
> "People in tales *don't* know, always. But there they are." (17)

Smoky, who never accepts the magic, nonetheless recognizes eventually that he has wandered into narrative: "it didn't seem that *they* minded, that I didn't believe in them, the Tale went on and all, just the same—didn't it?" (404) He knows that for Alice the Tale is as much home as is Edgewood, and he hopes he has been accepted into the one as he has into the other. As if to confirm his belief that his world has been absorbed into a narrative, another character muses on reasons for a dismal turn of events in "the world or this Tale (if there was a difference)" (432).

Late in the story, Smoky is distressed to feel the Tale winding to an ending that he fears will exclude him:

> No no no no. Things don't have ends like that, Alice. Any more than they have beginnings. Things are all middles in life. Like Auberon's show. Like history. One damn thing after another, that's all. (449)

But to Alice, being in a tale complete with beginning and ending is to hold life complete in one's understanding:

How could it be, Daily Alice wondered as they kissed, that to say such things as she had said to the husband she loved, on this darkest night of the year, made her not sad but glad, filled in fact with happy expectation? The end: to have the Tale end meant to her to have it all forever, no part left out, complete and seamless at last—certainly Smoky couldn't be left out, not as deeply woven into its stuff as he had become. It would be good, so good to have it all at last, start to finish, like some long, long piece of work that has been executed in dribs and dabs, in the hope and faith that the last nail, the last stitch, the last tug at the strings, will make it all suddenly make sense: what a relief! (452)

A relief and a wonder: Crowley has, through Alice, just summed up the way fantasy imposes structure and therefore wonder on experience. In achieving this understanding, Alice has qualified herself to replace "them" as the shaper of her own tale. She can invent her own happy ending, but that ending will, in some respects, remarkably resemble tragedy. Even as a storyteller, Daily Alice will find herself constrained by the needs of the Tale itself.

So, indeed, was her predecessor among "them." Mrs. Underhill, who governs both world and story since she is a combination of Mother Goose and Mother Nature, with a bit of the Red Queen thrown in for spice, can't tell what the tale means. "If I'd known more than I said I'd have said it," is her answer to Violet Drinkwater, who has been suffering from one of Mrs. Underhill's prophecies (52). Nor can she say whether the Tale has a happy ending: "Well who's to say. . . . It's a Tale, is all. There are only short ones and long ones. Yours is the longest *I* know" (53).

Little, Big combines the internal consistency of Tolkienian fantasy with the burgeoning, unpredictable invention of Postmodernism. It manages to satisfy us as a well-executed fairy tale while challenging us to discover whence fairy tales arise and why we never cease to need them.

Despite these pleasures, however, the novel has received little attention outside the small circle of fantasy scholars. Fans of formula fantasy find it puzzling, while the audience for more complex fictions either has not heard of it (no review appeared in any literary journal) or is put off by the fantasy framework. The case is much different with a very similar work, Mark Helprin's *Winter's Tale* (1983).

This novel, also a fairy tale set in New York and upcountry, also spanning a century or more, also densely allusive, also transforming American artifacts into magic (the resemblances between the two novels go so far as to include similar treatments of the zodiac on the ceiling of Grand Central Station), got the kind of attention *Little, Big* failed to receive two years earlier, including a front-page review in the *New York Times Book Review*. Yet it is a less inventive book than Crowley's, more monotonous in tone and style, less complex in theme. Its very real charm begins to wear thin somewhere in the last three or four hundred pages. It suffers from the same kind of pulling back, the same lack of authorial commitment that characterizes *Lanark* and *Chimera*.

Reviews of *Winter's Tale* show that readers classed it with Postmodernist fictions: it was seen as "fable," as "myth," as "magic realism," but not generally as "fantasy." Reviewers saw what they expected to see based on Helprin's earlier work, which was sometimes fantastic but generally within the bounds of mainstream fiction. *Little, Big,* on the other hand, was published as fantasy, by a publishing house with a considerable list of science fiction and fantasy, and its author had previously written works of straight science fiction and of the hybrid form, science fantasy, that has begun to dominate the popular market. Helprin's book, though a best-seller, was accordingly literature, while Crowley's was popular fiction.

One of the great accomplishments of Postmodernism, however, has been to break down such distinctions, resulting in what Fredric Jameson calls "aesthetic populism," defined as:

> the effacement . . . of the older (essentially high-modernist) frontier be-
> tween high culture and so-called mass or commercial culture, and the
> emergence of new kinds of texts infused with the forms, categories and
> contents of that very Culture Industry so passionately denounced by all the
> ideologues of the modern, from Leavis and the American New Criticism
> all the way to Adorno and the Frankfurt School. The postmodernists have
> in fact been fascinated precisely by this whole "degraded" landscape of
> schlock and kitsch, of TV series and Reader's Digest culture, of advertising
> and motels, of the late show and the grade-B Hollywood film, of so-called
> paraliterature with its airport paperback categories of the gothic and the
> romance, the popular biography, the murder mystery and the science-
> fiction or fantasy novel: materials they no longer simply "quote," as a Joyce
> or a Mahler might have done, but incorporate into their very substance.
> ("Postmodernism" 54–55)

Not only does literary Postmodernism draw upon popular forms, but its greatest works, such as Eco's *The Name of the Rose* or García Marquez's *One Hundred Years of Solitude,* are also popular successes. They draw freely on the storytelling arts that make reading a pleasure: adventure, mystery, suspense, and magic. In order to establish license to do so, they frequently issue disclaimers about the seriousness of their enterprise, saying that they are merely playing with language and the signs that derive from it. Theirs is not the high seriousness of the Modernists.

Such modesty about their aims may be a clever ploy, a bone to distract the watchdog critics so that they may go about their business unobserved. What is that business? Italo Calvino gives the game away in his essay

"Myth in the Narrative" (1975). Story, not meaning, is primary, he says. The first storytellers combined and recombined simple actions and familiar actors until their own internal logic asserted itself, with magic central to the process:

> Each animal, object, and relationship acquired beneficent or maleficent powers, which were to be called magical powers and should instead have been called narrative powers, potentials inherent in words, the faculty of combining with other words at the level of discourse. (76)

But inherent in this process, he says, is the possibility that a story can take on significance. The tribal storyteller "goes on permuting jaguars and toucans until there comes a moment when one of his innocent little stories explodes into a terrible revelation: a myth, which demands to be recited in secret and in a sacred place" (79). In Calvino's view, then, meaning in literature is not the result of dutiful recording of perceived reality, but of letting narrative formula shape natural phenomena, lending order and value to experience. The storytellers of our own particular tribe also need to "indulge in a playful attitude, a combinatorial game that may at a certain stage take on preconscious content and finally give it voice" (81).

The same playful attitude informs the work of Postmodernist architects like Robert Venturi and Michael Graves and composers like David Del Tredici, who has made a career out of musical settings of *Alice in Wonderland* the way earlier composers mined scripture or Romantic verse. When Del Tredici makes use of tonality and Graves alludes to classic architectural orders, they do so in a surprising fashion that could be called fantastic. They know these are neither divinely ordained systems, as the nineteenth century thought, nor exhausted formalisms, as the early twentieth century believed, but "combinatorial games" that can occasionally generate meaning. The critical theories that validate their work also change our perspective on the past, justifying in retrospect the seeming conservatism of a Maybeck or a Vaughan Williams.

Just so, Postmodernism justifies the practice of fantasists, who have always been willing to play with the inconsequential until it explodes into myth. So, too, fantasists like Crowley bear out the theories of Postmodernists by generating stories in which we recognize the parts of ourselves that defy any other means of analysis.

FOUR

Fantasy and Narrative Conventions: Story

FICTION, LIKE STAGE MAGIC, is an act of collusion between performer and audience. The storyteller pulls a clump of sentences out of his hat, waves a wand, and tells us that those sentences have turned into people, scenes, and events. And we say, yes, I see it all. Unless the storyteller is extraordinarily incompetent or insistent on letting us in on his secrets, we are more than willing to be fooled. We prefer the pleasures of illusion to the smugness of skepticism.

This point needs to be made from time to time—Shakespeare reminds us of it frequently, so that we will attend to our duties as audience. Still, critics forget that even our best characters—Emma Woodhouse or Emma Bovary—are but shadows, while the worst are capable of walking us through a story if we can relate them to the appropriate narrative convention.

Conventions are the terms of agreement between writer and reader. Plot, character, setting, point of view—the writer agrees to organize his narrative around such landmarks, while we in return agree to supply the remembered images, knowledge of human behavior, and reading experience necessary to put flesh on the bones and make them move. Though we read only words, we experience places, personalities, and a passage of time unrelated to the duration of our reading.

We tend to forget that this is not an involuntary participation, like the perceptual blurring that makes a series of projected stills into a moving picture. Realistic fiction in particular emphasizes the author's role in generating the narrative illusion—it becomes a product of her "authority." In the critical theorizing that arose in response to the realist movement, tricks of the trade such as consistency of character, limited point of view, and the piling on of circumstantial evidence came to be viewed as ends in themselves. They were thought to be sufficient, as if the reader had no choice but to believe and be moved.

And so arose a critical orthodoxy which ranked the covertly conventional novel above the explicitly conventional romance. In the name of realism, conventions like the symmetrical plot were devalued as organizing principles for fiction. Dickens's plots were an embarrassment, something he, as a Great Author, should have outgrown. Walter Scott might just as well have stuck to the law. E. M. Forster is a typical, though late, spokesman of the realist program. Plot, he says, is "a fetish, borrowed from the drama, from the spatial limitations of the stage" (97). But plot, by which he means a conception of the story's events as a function of character interaction, is partially redeemed by its connection with the portrayal of motivations. Plot can divert the audience from mere curiosity into a consideration of values. It can teach us to ask "Why?" instead of the untutored response of "And then?" (86). There is no such justification for story itself. In constructing a story, the writer is giving in to the reader's impertinent demands to know what happened next, rather than expressing her vision of human nature.

"I wish it were not so," Forster says: that instead of being bound to the convention of storymaking, the novelist could build on "something different—melody, or the perception of the truth, not this low atavistic form" (26).

The trouble with this desire, as Forster recognized, is that it leads the writer out the other side of realism. A narrative freed from convention turns out to be even less capable of rendering experience faithfully than the most conventional romance: "The time sequence cannot be destroyed without carrying in its ruin all that should have taken its place; the novel that would express values only becomes unintelligible and therefore valueless" (42).

A number of writers in this century have done what Forster dared not do, writing novels without characters, without motivations, without sequence, without values. Experimental novelists like Nathalie Sarraute, Samuel Beckett, Philippe Sollers, and Alain Robbe-Grillet have effectively destroyed the conventional illusions of narrative, leaving the audience to stare at bare wires and mirrors. Such non-stories assert that there is no real mimesis, no representation possible through the arbitrary sign-system of language, perhaps no communicable reality at all, but only the manipulation of black shapes on the white page.

This attempt to dismantle narrative convention is a natural, though unexpected, outgrowth of the realist enterprise. Those words on the page are, after all, the only real thing the novelist can offer. In contrast, the literature of unreality has provided a rationale for reconstructing the elements of fiction. Instead of viewing storytelling as an unavoidable necessity, a distasteful chore for the novelist really interested in reproducing reality or in making a statement, some contemporary writers and critics are learning to see narrative conventions as the grammatical rules for a distinctive mode of discourse. Writers are making use of the fantastic to investigate the way narrative, in a two-way partnership between speaker and listener like that of language, creates the realities it seems merely to reflect.

If I were speaking only of the elusive, erudite, self-referential fictions of Borges and Calvino, I would merely be repeating conventional wisdom. But fantasies at every level of complexity share this ability to remake fiction. Naive, no less than postmodernist, fantasies are capable of forcing the reader to reconsider the process of telling and reading stories. The only difference is that the pose of sophistication pushes a narrative toward preciosity and self-doubt while naiveté—or the deliberate imitation of a naive storytelling stance—tends to reconfirm the conventions that make narration a potentially meaningful form of discourse.

Another way of looking at the issues discussed in the last chapter is to say that the postmodern fantastic, by adopting a playful stance toward narrative conventions, forces the reader to take an active part in establishing any coherence and closure within the text, thereby strengthening the conventional contract. But the same may be said about many other kinds of fantastic literature, including some formula novels and fantasies written for children. Even the simplest of fantasies sets up an initial paradox on the order of "everything I tell you is a lie, including this." The blatancy of this untruth deconstructs the text before it begins—in a fairy tale, the words "once upon a time" really mean never, upon no time. From this paradox grows fantasy's potential for reinvigorating narrative forms. Unlike more sophisticated genres, fantasy can be self-referential without being self-destructive; artificial without being arch.

"Once upon a time" also signals the importance of time itself in fantasy. Narrative is language's way of exploring time; it enables us to give shape and meaning to time in somewhat the same way architecture orders space. The literary convention we call story is our way of establishing imaginative control over time, and so is the fundamental vehicle for artistry within narrative discourse.

Yet critics like Forster have for centuries undervalued story, reserving their praise for elegant or innovative style or the interaction of characters—as if they were reading poetry or watching a play, rather than reading fiction. The first critics to pay close attention to writers' manipulation of time were the structuralists. Vladimir Propp, Northrop Frye, Gérard Genette, and Robert Scholes have looked not only at fiction from the last two centuries but also at traditional forms such as myth, legend, epic, and folktale, in an attempt to devise systems for comprehending the compelling flow of discovery, transformation, confrontation, and reconciliation that characterizes all narrative, from the epic of Gilgamesh to Calvino's metafictions. Genette, particularly, has investigated the writer's strategies for controlling the passage of narrative time. Developed in response to *Remembrance of Things Past*—Proust's exhaustive attempt to explore through fiction the complex interaction of memory and time— Genette's structural schema shows how the writer can accelerate or retard the pace, anticipate the future or return to previous moments, treat multiple events as one or rerun a single event many times. Though Genette is working with an example of essentially realistic fiction, his system can be used to analyze the effect of a fantastic frame on our perception of time.

Fantastic tales are generally seen as naive or artless because they emphasize story over verbal texture and depth of characterization. This is true of the oral predecessors of modern fantasy and is equally true of a work like *The Lord of the Rings*. Tolkien's language varies between everyday speech and an archaic and formal rhetoric. His characters are patterned after received types—the wizard, the lady, the comic servant— and reveal themselves primarily through appearance and action. His presentation of events is governed by the rhetorical structure of a folktale, which, as Genette points out, "habitually conforms, at least in its major articulations, to chronological order" (36).

This narrative conservatism, however, must be reexamined from the vantage point of structuralist theory and post-structuralist glosses on it. These last alert us to discontinuities within a text, which may function as an independent code in which an underlying discourse comments upon or even contradicts surface-level assertions. And what do we find underlying fantasy's narrative conventionality? A continuous implied assertion that everyday language lies, that coherent characters are inventions of the observer, and especially that orderliness and chronology properly belong to the realm of the imagination.

Fantasy is generally defined in terms of a violation of expectations: prominent within a work of fantasy is some element of the *im*possible or *super*natural, the writer relying on our consensus as to the nature of the possible or natural within the world of nonliterary experience. Hence, in this view, the violation occurs at the level of reference.

The referential status of fantasy bears close attention, and C. S. Lewis,

C. N. Manlove, Kathryn Hume, and others have proposed valuable approaches to its investigation. Yet one can also look at the impossibilities that make fantasy fantastic, not as they are defined against consensus reality, but as they affect the conventional elements of narrative. This chapter examines fantasy's redefinition of story, or the fictional representation of time; implications regarding the convention of character will be considered in the next.

The impossible in fantasy is generally codified. Magical operations are grouped into principles resembling natural law: shape shifters must conserve mass in transforming, knowledge of names gives power over things. And uses of magic are governed by ethical strictures: one is responsible for the forces one unleashes. Magic is indeed not merely codified: it is itself a code as old as language, or older. It is as rule-bound as language and, like language, extends its realm through metonymy and metaphor, also known as contagion and similarity.

This magical code is accepted in a work of fantasy as part of its fictional ground rules, one of the defining characteristics of its universe. Once admitted to the fictional world, however, magic works to redefine everything else. In particular, the magical code allows the author to send messages about narrative sequence, about character, and about the ontological status of narrative statements, or, in other words, about the boundary between the fictional and the real.

Essential to any narrative is a series of events arranged into an orderly sequence of before and after, cause and effect. It is the narrator's prerogative to scramble that order. She may begin in the middle, use flashback to fill us in on prior events, and hint at outcomes in order to heighten or flatten suspense. These, however, are perceived as literary devices—choices on the narrator's part that leave unaltered the flow of incidents.

What does magic do to narrative time? A writer of fantasy can, of course, make use of every violation of continuous flow of narrative time that Genette identifies in his study of Proust: jumps backward or forward; ellipses, summaries, and pauses; repeated retellings of a single event or the compression of multiple events into one by using iterative verb forms and adverbial markers such as *would go, often, every day.*

But most fantasies avoid these devices, which are perceived as part of the discourse of the narrative rather than alterations of the story itself. Because they are encoded into the text as authorial interventions, ellipses and pauses and repetitions have no effect on our perception of the actual sequence of events. But the fantasist has the option of disrupting time at the level of story. Time itself may be described as jumping, pausing, repeating, or looping back on itself as a result of magical operations. There is even precedent for the distortion of story time in folk narratives, which often portray time in Elfland as running at a different rate than human time, with tragic results to the unlucky mortal who crosses the boundary.

An instance of a more complete disruption of time is found in a comic fantasy—a formula story of a sort that might be called "gadget fantasy"— by John D. MacDonald, called *The Girl, the Gold Watch, and Everything* (1962). The story describes a watch with the power to halt the passage of time for everything in the universe except the possessor of the device. The result is a split: we now have not one but two independent time streams. From the universe's point of view, the watch allows the protagonist to move about instantaneously. For the protagonist, people and actions around him are frozen, letting him examine and even alter the scene to his own satisfaction.

Though MacDonald uses this effect primarily as a way of generating a formulaic plot, magical violations of time sequence may also function as a way of calling our attention to two important narrative conventions. One of these permits the storyteller to pass quickly over a chunk of time, either because nothing is happening that relates to the chosen narrative or because something *is* happening but the reader is not to be told about it until afterwards. The other convention allows a character to pause and observe a scene, often in great detail, while no action takes place. Neither is possible in real life. Both operations begin to take effect when we transform experience into narrative in the form of memory. By placing them on the same level as the events on which they operate, fantasy encourages us to examine their role in constructing the version of events we choose to remember.

The great Edwardian children's writer E. Nesbit explored several forms of magical disruption of time sequence. A rigorous pursuer of the logical implications of magic (and a friend of the great time traveler, H. G. Wells), Nesbit was especially alert to its capacity to generate paradox. The logic of time is most evident in her paired novels *The House of Arden* (1908) and *Harding's Luck* (1910). In *Harding's Luck,* for instance, Dickie Harding divides his time between the twentieth century and the seventeenth. Days spent in the earlier life take no time in the later; like the operations of MacDonald's gold watch, these periods correspond to pauses in a nonmagical narrative. But when Dickie tries to send money to his later self, the times begin to impinge on one another. From then on, time spent in 1906 is somehow used up in Dickie's absence in 1606. (Nesbit may be commenting on our way of seeing time as money, to be spent or saved or borrowed. Dickie has sold part of his time to gain cash.) Dickie, like the reader, experiences these missing periods as narrative ellipses, which must be filled by the summaries provided by his nurse.

Nesbit proposes another set of time-traveling children, Dickie's cousins Edred and Elfrida Arden, who overlap with Dickie in both seventeenth and twentieth centuries. These two, however, do not necessarily experience events in the same sequence as Dickie, so that what is a flashback for him might be prolepsis, or a flashforward, for them. Furthermore, Edred and Elfrida, who have some schooling in history, tend to see the past as essentially less real than the present. Nesbit emphasizes its pageant-like quality, in their eyes, by having their time-traveling triggered by a game of dressing up in costumes of the appropriate era. Elfrida, heading into Queen Anne's time, thinks, "It was like going into a dream. Nothing would be real there" (*The House of Arden* 79).

Memory, even partial memory of history learned in school, seems to operate as a barrier between perceiver and experience. In another adventure, Elfrida accidentally gives away the Gunpowder Plot before it has come off, but she cannot quite believe that her actions can change the past: "This is James the First's time, and I'm in it. But it's three hundred years ago all the same, and it all *has* happened, and it can't make any difference what I say . . ." (141).

But to Dickie, who in the twentieth century is an impoverished orphan with no chance for studying history, the past has not yet happened, and therefore is as real as the present. He finds a place and an identity in the seventeenth century, whereas his cousins are never more than tourists in any past time. When he and they coincide for the first time, his reaction is "I don't like it," because "it makes it seem not real. It's only a dream, really, I suppose. And I'd got to believe that it was really real" (*Harding's Luck* 174).

Nesbit plays a number of games with dreams and reality, past and future, memory and duration. She even makes use of the magic of time travel to replay a scene from *The House of Arden* in its sequel, but from another point of view, altering its perceived outcome and significance. In order to dovetail the two narratives, she must stop time for some characters and accelerate it for others. Dickie, for instance, must live through seven months of 1907 in order to catch up with his cousins, and those seven months are longer than the three hundred years he has already come. In both books, the orderliness of narrative flow is completely disrupted by events accounted for within the narrative, with no overt intervention from the storyteller.

Diana Wynne Jones, in many ways a latter-day Nesbit, introduces a further complication in narrative time. In *Archer's Goon* (1984), events that we believe are happening for the first time are revealed to be on their third go round. The span from the protagonist's infancy to age twelve has been twice reenacted, once because of his accidental interference, the

second time deliberately. Each time, however, new elements are introduced, so the reiteration of events is not exact. Otherwise the loop would
be forever closed, the twelve years lived through endlessly. Enough remains constant, though, that the entire story could be told in present or
future tense as appropriately as in the past tense: the story's opening could
well read, "The trouble begins/ will begin the day Howard comes/ was
coming/ had come/ will have been coming home from school to find the
Goon sitting in the kitchen." Though Jones avoids such *nouveau roman*
experiments and renders her unconventional time scheme in conventional
tense, by the end of the book, the reader has been alerted to the possibilities. Our initial perceptions have been effectively deconstructed.

One of the elements that alters the twelve-year cycle is the memory of
previous trips through it. Various characters possess or have access to such
memories according to their degree of magical talent and according to
whether they are caught within its limited sphere of operation. A character named Erskine, for instance, can move outside the geographical limits
of the time bubble, while Hathaway "lives in the past" (a phrase the
protagonist initially takes as a figure of speech). Thus they both come to
remember more than anyone else, though Howard, who has pulled everyone back through time with him, seems to have an unconscious awareness
of his prior actions.

These memories, since they cover a twelve-year period that has not, in
its current run-through, completely elapsed, can function paradoxically
as prophecies: This will happen because it has happened. And, like all
prophecies, a memory may bring about its own fulfillment or, in Jones's
less deterministic universe, invalidate itself because it changes the balance
of forces.

Prophecy has always been a major channel for magic's infringement on
narrative time. Whether these prophecies issue from a character like T. H.
White's Merlin as he moves backward through time or from gods or fates
existing outside of time, such intrusions of future into present or past
(many fictional prophecies are "ancient") reveal just how arbitrary is the
choice to imitate the one-way passage of real time in a piece of narrative
art. All suspense, all dramatic irony, every effect that depends on the
reader's or characters' ignorance of the future is dependent on this literary
convention, which has grown stale because we take it for granted. But
fantasy, by not allowing us to assume, revitalizes the convention.

Jones herself comments on fantasy's ability to alter narrative time in an
article on "The Shape of the Narrative in *The Lord of the Rings*" (1983).
Jones was a student of Tolkien, in two senses. She describes her experience
as an undergraduate at Oxford, when she attended his course on narrative. Despite his less than inspiring lecture style—he spoke nearly inau-

dibly, she says, and "when it did appear that we might be hearing what he said, it was his custom to turn round and address the blackboard" (87)— she came away with "inklings" of the possibilities of narrative development, which developed into a fuller understanding after she compared his comments with his own practice:

> The plot of *The Lord of the Rings* is, on the face of it, exactly the same simple one he appeared to describe in his lectures: a journey that acquires an aim and develops into a kind of quest. But the bare plot is to any writer no more than the main theme of a sort of symphony which requires other themes added to it and the whole orchestrated into a narrative. To shape a narrative, you have to phase the various incidents and so control their nature that you set up significances, correspondences, foretastes and expectations, until your finished story becomes something else again from its simple outline. Tolkien does this orchestrating supremely well . . . . (88)

In other words, Tolkien has managed to complicate the beginning-to-end chronology of the fairy tale without violating it. Some of the devices Tolkien uses to turn a simple story into temporal counterpoint are available to the writer of realistic fiction. Yet we are uncomfortable when a primarily mimetic story calls too often upon coincidence, foreshadowing, oracular pronouncements, or repetition of patterns. We see the author's hand too plainly at work, the card up the sleeve. But when Tolkien and Jones set up prophecies or parallel events, they do so within the context of a magical world, in which coincidence and correspondence have the force of natural law.

Jones points out how each major movement in *LOTR* is followed by what she calls a "coda," in which prior events are reconsidered and future ones anticipated (88). The end of the stay at Bree, for instance, is signaled by Frodo's putting on the Ring and disappearing under the table. This is parallel to Bilbo's earlier disappearing act at the birthday party, but the hobbits are no longer in the safe Shire. In the Inn with them are large, unpredictable Men and spies of Mordor. "The fact that he puts the Ring on while singing a nursery rhyme only underlines the fact that such things are now inappropriate" (93). Indeed, Frodo's seemingly innocent action leads to a precipitate flight from Bree, leading directly to the confrontation with the Ringwraiths on Weathertop. We begin to see that things were not quite so simple even the first time in the Shire, for the Ringwraiths were there, too, sniffing around. And, if we are alert, we anticipate yet another instance of putting on the Ring, when a no longer naive Frodo intentionally disappears from the Fellowship to go his way alone. Each parallel movement effectively rewrites those that went before. Each prepares the way for those yet to come. The explicit prophecies and embedded narratives merely reinforce the intricate structuring of the narrative, pointing out to the reader the way the magic code governs the unfolding of events.

Furthermore, the characters in *LOTR* are surrounded by emblems of the past and omens of the future; in other words, time takes concrete form. One such form is the River Anduin. Time and rivers have a long metaphoric association, but Tolkien's use of the image is unusual, as Jones points out:

> This Anduin has contrasting banks and, moreover, reeks of history. In a way, it *is* history, and the Fellowship is going with its current, to break up in confusion at the falls of Rauros. It is worth pointing out that when Aragorn later uses the same river, he comes *up* it, against the current, changing a course of events that seems inevitable. (98)

Two other images relate to time. If the river is history, the sea is eternity, or, as Jones says, "both all time and no time at all" (98). And the Eye of Sauron, in the arid land at the farthest remove from the Sea, can be seen, "among its various significances, as the eye of the storm, the self-contained here-and-now, which the present has to pass through before it becomes the future" (98).

These are not merely different moments in time, but rival conceptions of time: the transfixing of time by the Eye must be rejected, the conventional time of the River must be endured, and the transcendence of time represented by the Sea may be hoped for. These conceptions of time are also conceptions of the Self, from Sauron's all-embracing selfishness to Frodo's self-sacrifice, which wins him a place in the last sea-going ship.

In addition to the concrete symbols that Jones points out, Tolkien also uses the various peoples of Middle-earth to represent different ways of relating to time. His elves, for instance, do not age. Death comes to them only through accident or violence. A major source of the eerie melancholy that pervades Tolkien's creation is the occasional glimpse he gives us of an elvish perspective on time. Elves are surrounded by short-lived creatures. Some of the latter, like humankind, resemble elves and can even intermarry with them, but always with tragic results, for the mortal partner must die and the immortal face an eternity of bereavement. The elves have eons to refine their arts, but they know that anything made by them will crumble before their eyes, including great fortresses like Gondolin and enchanted woods like Lothlorien. Therefore they concentrate, in latter days, on song and speech, which are ephemeral and yet outlast monuments.

Whereas Tolkien's men are tempted into sin by the hope of outwitting death, the elves fall through their attempts to arrest change. They see all victories as Pyrrhic, all joys as echoes of earlier glories. Their Golden Age is no myth but an ever-receding memory.

In addition to this elvish conception of time, Tolkien also lets us see the world through the eyes of the ents, who, with the life span of bristlecone pines, mediate between ageless elves and hasty hobbits. Going even beyond the elves, there is Tom Bombadil, the Eldest, who predates creation. Whereas they are wise and weary, he, who knows no beginnings or ends, is full of merriment and foolery. His time is a continuous renewal of rainfall and wildflowers, of otter-play and water flowing.

Each of these conceptions of time is conveyed most clearly through the narratives of the various peoples: the falling cadences of the elves' songs, Treebeard's lengthy and long-lined verse, the hobbits' nursery tales, Tom Bombadil's way of narrating his own actions even as he performs them, as if every moment were a sort of rhyme fulfilling the moment before. Each deconstructs the others but does not invalidate them. Hobbit-time is as real as demigod-time. How you see it depends on where you stand to look. Rather than pretending to represent some sort of "real time," therefore, fantasy allows for a number of different, even contradictory conceptions of the nature and meaning of time, no one of which is privileged above the others.

But implied in the ending of *LOTR* is the replacement of this variety by the human notion of history, which is linear, uniform, and scaled to the human life span. Tolkien's example shows that one effective strategy for reconstructing narrative time is to transform one sort of time—not merely past, present, and future but a distinctive way of ordering and interpreting time—into another through the action of the narrative. E. Nesbit hints at a similar reordering in *Harding's Luck,* when Dickie's old Nurse informs him that time as he understands it, historical time, is not real: "But there's seasons, and the season they came out of was summer, and the season you'll go back to 'tis autumn . . ." (183). Dickie ultimately abandons the twentieth century, in which seasons are largely ignored, for the seventeenth, in which they are the fundamental rhythm of life. In *Archer's Goon,* too, one vision of time is replaced by another, when the closed circuit gives way to an open-ended future.

In Ursula K. Le Guin's *The Tombs of Atuan* (1971), magic converts cyclic time, the eternal return of myth, into linear, historical time. In the process, Arha, the ever-reborn priestess of the nameless ones, becomes Tenar, a unique individual in an unprecedented situation. Conversely, Crowley's *Little, Big* follows its characters as they drop out of history into eternity. Crowley signals the shift by naming his heroine Daily Alice, at first a nickname for Alice Dale but by the end a description of her role as mother goddess who recreates the world daily.

Jones puts her understanding of the temporal organization of narrative to fullest use in her novel *Fire and Hemlock* (1985). Having discovered from Tolkien how to make a single narrative moment refer simultaneously backward and forward in time, she demonstrates how his technique can become the basis for an entire story. The relationship of present to past is introduced first, as the heroine uncovers a set of buried memories overlaid by a false past. At the beginning of the story, Polly, packing for her second year of college, comes across a book called *Times out of Mind*. One of the stories in the book, called "Two-Timer," sounds a bit like *Archer's Goon*: "it was about someone who went back in time to his own childhood and changed things, so that his life ran differently the second time" (4). Polly remembers reading the story, and Jones sneaks a sly bit of metafiction into her judgment: "The man finished by having two sets of memories, and the story wasn't worked out at all well" (4). But other things about the book disturb her: "Half the stories she thought she remembered reading in this book were not there—and yet she did, very clearly, remember reading all the stories which seemed to be in the book now" (4).

Rereading the book leads her into reminiscence, and the memories that emerge, like those of the man whose story she did not like, are double. Most of the narration in *Fire and Hemlock* is what would be called a flashback in a more conventional novel, but in this case is clearly an advancement of the plot. For Polly, it is the recovery of the five years when she was in contact with a man named Thomas Lynn, who has been erased from her mind and the memories of those around her. As she remembers events from those years, they lead her to mementos which trigger further memories—objects, like the book, that have been mysteriously altered or that fit awkwardly into the present situation derived from the false memories she has been given.

The more Polly remembers, the closer she comes to understanding now and why her past has become falsified by the sinister Laurel or Lorelei Perry. Laurel is the Queen of Elfland, and Thomas Lynn is her latest mortal lover and victim, like his namesakes in balladry Thomas the Rhymer and Tam Lin. In coming to understand the situation, Polly also determines her future, for she is the only one who can rescue Tom. Thus, each step in her search changes the events that led up to it; moreover, these alterations of the past change the nature of the task foreordained for her.

The key to recovering the past and reaching a successful conclusion lies in the generation of narrative. In addition to the narrative that Polly tells herself as she reconstructs the missing years, several other narratives are essential to the construction of *Fire and Hemlock*. There is the story that sets her to remembering, of course, which in the revised past is part of a collection written by Tom Lynn and the other members of his string quartet. It is still "less good than any of the others" (211). Another story in the collection is called "Fire and Hemlock," which is also the title of a photograph on Polly's wall. This photograph, not surprisingly, holds stories within it, or used to before Laurel's magic altered it:

> Dark figures had seemed to materialize out of its dark center—strong, running dark figures—always at least four of them, racing to beat out the flames in the foreground. There had been times when you could see the figures quite clearly. Other times, they had been shrouded in the rising smoke. There had even been a horse in it sometimes. (3)

In addition, fire and hemlock constitute the ingredients of the spell with which Polly pulls disaster down on herself.

The narratives of the two ballads mentioned above provide Polly with important clues to the narrative in which she finds herself. As she reviews the past, she realizes that Tom Lynn's gifts of books frequently have disguised such clues: he has sent her innumerable fantasies, stories of King Arthur, the book in which she finds the ballads, *The Golden Bough,* and a collection of fairy tales, of which he says, "Only thin, weak thinkers despise fairy stories. Each one has a true, strange fact hidden in it, you know, which you can find if you look" (117).

Besides providing clues about his enslavement by Laurel, these books exercise Polly's imagination, which is important because any hope of freeing him depends on a game he and Polly play, in which she invents a story that is and is not about them both. That is, it is a fantasy, in which he is a hero named Tan Coul and she is his apprentice. They begin to invent the story together when they first meet, and continue it in letters. He realizes, though she does not, that the things they invent come true—the Queen of Elfland has given him the same gift she gave Thomas Rhymer, of speaking nothing but truth. So when he discusses with Polly her ideas about Tan Coul's horse, his three co-heroes, or his search for a magical implement called the Obah Cypt, he insures that those things will come to pass. The other heroes, for instance, show up as the musicians who will help him form his string quartet. (They call themselves the Dumas Quartet, in reference to yet another narrative.) The four heroes are the four figures in the *Fire and Hemlock* picture, and the other members of the quartet support Tom and Polly in the final showdown. The stories thus constitute the only means of diverging from Laurel's plans for Tom's future as a sacrificial victim.

In *Fire and Hemlock,* time is a spell, and spells are stories, and stories are the only way to pin time down and make it behave. There are levels to the book that I have not touched on, including a second invented history for Tan Coul and his assistant that also comes true, but in a completely different fashion. Many clues are also offered to the reader about how a story may be constructed out of other stories without merely imitating them. When Polly discovers Tolkien, for instance—on her own, not a gift from Tom—she decides the Obah Cypt must be a dangerous magic ring. But Tom realizes the magic of narrative cannot work that way: he responds with a postcard saying, "No, it's not a ring. You stole that from Tolkien. Use your own ideas" (127). Whereas Polly's earlier mixture of half-remembered, and thus wholly original, motifs was of service to Tom, her attempt to draw directly from another tale is doomed to failure.

This fantasy, so intricately constructed as to defy summary; so full of metafictional devices; so Proustian, one might say, in its transformations of sequence, order, and duration—this novel was published for young readers. If such readers are sufficiently well read to recognize its use of the fairy tale structure of quest and qualified happy ending, they should have no trouble in either following the tale to its conclusion or in absorbing its lessons in narrative art. Like Tolkien, Jones is educating her audience in the conventions that allow fixed words on a page to simulate the passage of time. As the audience learns to participate, these conventions are reinvigorated, and the possibilities for further narrative invention are enhanced.

Furthermore, because a work of fantasy must by (my) definition reach a successful conclusion, must resolve whatever dilemmas it raises in such a way that gains, however slimly, exceed losses, it can comment obliquely on the role of conventions in other kinds of narrative. Most particularly, fantasies can alter our sense of an ending.

When John Crowley transforms time into a mythic eternity at the end of *Little, Big,* he also places his characters at the same level of narrative reality with time itself, for Father Time, complete with hourglass and scythe, makes a brief appearance in the book. Daily Alice and all who accompany her through the final transformation become the equals of Time and thus no longer subject to time in its most disturbing aspect: death.

Since the story of every living being has the same ending, a mimetic narrator has two choices for ending his story. He can follow characters to their deaths or stop short of the final scene. Strictly realistic works must, therefore, either end tragically or inconclusively. Such conventional endings as the discovery of treasure, a long-deferred reunion, the capture of a criminal, or a marriage always leave the possibility of asking E. M. Forster's "And then?" If we accept these events as conclusions it is because they satisfy our sense of story, not of mimesis. As the modern equivalents of "They lived happily ever after," they mark forms like the detective novel as modern versions of romance. From a realist's point of view they represent compromise, a necessary evil, like the need to maintain audience interest through suspense.

But such devices are the basis of the fantasist's art form. The beginning of a fantasy already implies an ending that is, by realist standards, contrived—one that will provide for all characters and answer all questions. This is one reason that good fantasy is difficult to write, and that many writers evade their responsibility by borrowing an ending from Tolkien or elsewhere. The fact that the ending must be implied in the beginning complicates the task further, for if there is no surprise, there is no reason to read on. But the best fantasies do what Jones says Tolkien does:

> you are told, this early on, exactly what is going to happen. And you are still in doubt that it will. Each of the Fellowship of the Ring says exactly what his intentions are, and yet you do not believe they will do as they say. Each time I read it, I am still pained and shocked when the Fellowship divides later on. I am still in doubt that the Ring will be destroyed, or what good it would do if it was. It seems to me to need some explaining how Tolkien got away with it. (94)

One explanation is that although the ending is what we expect, its meaning is unexpected. We expect that Frodo will destroy the Ring and return to the Shire, but we do not realize that he will do so only by becoming a different sort of being: a hero, with the grandeur and the tragic overtones that all true heroes have. Yet we should have known that only a hero can fulfill a heroic task. The ending is there, but only the passage of narrative time allows us to see it as we look back.

If mimetic storytelling is the witch who says, "Beauty will prick her finger and die," fantasy is the forgotten fairy who can step out of line to convert death into something stranger. Frodo passes away, like King Arthur, but he does not die. Ged, in Le Guin's *The Farthest Shore* (1972), journeys to the country of death and on beyond to life again. John Crowley's Smoky Barnable dies on the threshold of immortality but is there with Daily Alice all the same, is indeed an essential ingredient in the new world she creates. The magical code gives access to a whole range of alternative endings, of ways of reordering time.

Since an ending is a frame dividing the world of the story from that of the reader, to alter the nature of endings is to blur the boundaries. If magic can make things already reported not have happened, changing reality retroactively, or turn the inevitable into the unexpected, then it is not surprising that it can also violate the barrier separating the time represented in the narrative from the times of composing and reading the text.

Most fantasy writers provide clearly defined frames: narrative devices that establish a relationship between the fantasy world and our own while at the same time separating the two. These might consist of threshold stories, in which characters move from a realistic setting into another realm, or embedded narratives like Tolkien's Red Book of Westmarch, an imaginary text that presumably exists in our world and contains the records of Middle Earth.

Yet these frames, too, can be disrupted by magic. The framing device in Jones's *The Spell-Coats* (1979) is an unusual form of embedded narrative: a pair of woven garments whose stitches function as both words and spells, so that the coats are both the record of events and major elements within those events. The narrative is thus part of the story, a paradox that brings to the foreground such problems as selecting and ordering incidents in such a way as to reveal more than the storyteller herself knows. Closure, too, becomes a problem when the end of the story can only take place after the narrative—the woven coat—has been completed. Magic, which causes these problems, also solves them: the end of the story is revealed in a prophetic vision which only takes on its full meaning after the reader has finished reading: the ending is both inside and outside the narrative proper.

Thus magic can blur boundaries and question the status of fictional narrative itself. It can make the reader imaginatively enter the narrative fabric or give characters access to the storytelling process that has invented them. Jones illustrates the latter possibility in *Fire and Hemlock* and even more explicitly in *Archer's Goon,* where a typewriter on which anything typed becomes true (a not uncommon motif in fantasy) becomes a means for cutting through levels of reality:

> Quentin announced solemnly, "I now begin." Everyone was quiet while he tapped away at the keys. Howard watched the words coming over Quentin's shoulder. "The first to appear was Archer . . ."
>
> "Archer's coming!" Awful called from the window.
>
> Howard sped over there to look. Archer's Rolls was nosing its way through the main gates, silvery in the moonlight. Its headlights blazed across the light streaming from the door of the temple.
>
> " 'in his Rolls,' " Quentin murmured as he typed, " 'headlights . . . light from temple . . . ' " (234–35)

Is the story we are reading the same as the story Quentin is writing? Yes and no: the two keep converging, yet the characters' awareness that they are inventing the action keeps them apart, and keeps pushing one of those narrative levels in the direction of primary reality, the level at which we envision Diana Wynne Jones sitting at a similar typewriter inventing

Quentin and *his* typewriter. Yet that, too, is a fiction, a phantom narrative conjured up by the text, for Jones's act of invention is over, and for that matter, we do not know that she even used a typewriter to record it.

Because magic can bring embedded narratives up to the story's primary level of reality, as when the main characters in *Fire and Hemlock* come face to face with characters they had made up as a game, it is evident that virtually any metafictional device may be incorporated into fantasy at story level, as part of the workings of the magic that makes it fantastic. Legend may become history, past merge with future, and characters dictate their own fates, all without breaking the ground rules initially set and accepted by the reader.

Unlike realist texts, fantasies freely acknowledge their own disjunctions and deny at the outset any direct applicability of their fictional discourse to the realm of action and perception, but the result is not disorder and disillusionment.

Rather than leaving us in a solipsistic void, fantasy invites us to re-create what it has denied. As soon as it is announced that the world we are reading about bears no relation to our world, we begin to make connections. If physical rules have been altered beyond recognition, we look for moral rules. If we are confronted by a being whose appearance and powers deny its humanity, we begin to look for human motivations. If time is fragmented, reversed, or looped upon itself, then we are encouraged to exercise our own storytelling powers to draw a connection from beginning to end. By forcing a recognition of the arbitrariness of all such narrative conventions, fantasy reminds us of how useful they are, not only in literary sleight of hand, but also in formulating our own imaginative understanding of our existence in time, which can only be comprehended through narrative.

The pose of innocence, the seeming simplicity of most modern fantasy, is necessary for the success of the reconstructive function. As Fredric Jameson points out in a discussion of the related mode of science fiction, certain types of naiveté seem to coexist with "wide influence, historical importance . . . and even artistic quality and value. If this is so, then . . . we should inquire whether the formal possibility of a certain kind of aesthetic and narrative value may not rather *presuppose* and be dialectically related to just such otherwise seemingly oversimplified content" ("Science Fiction" 46).

Though some authors seem to be alarmed at the potentially disruptive nature of the fantastic, and hence retreat into the safe confines of formula, others have risen to the challenge. Tolkien, Jones, Crowley, and the like produce texts that look "readable," in the terminology of Derrida and Barthes, but that are, in their ultimate implications, "writable." They must be constructed, rewritten, assembled into meaningful order by the reader, who has been given a guide to the process in the very magical operations he is reading about.

By placing questions of memory and fate, cause and effect, invention and experience at the level of story, rather than leaving them at the discretion of a narrator as realistic fiction tends to do, fantasy suggests that they are central to the process of storytelling, and not mere stylistic choices. They operate at the level of narrative code, rather than of discourse. A realistic work is merely one that disguises the doubts built into its fictionality. By displaying rather than suppressing the arbitrariness of narrative choices, fantasy can breathe new life into its own conventions.

FIVE

Fantasy and Narrative Conventions: Character

A FICTIONAL CHARACTER is composed of a set of textual fragments scattered through a narrative. The most common of these are passages of description ascribed to a narrator or to other characters, passages summarizing actions, and passages of speech or internal commentary ascribed to the character herself. In the theater, an actor constructs a consistent conception of a character from similar fragments and attempts to embody it, lending the fictional construct the solidity of her physical presence and the continuity of her voice, features, and expressions. Our experience of Hedda Gabler or Blanche DuBois differs from our experience of real acquaintances only in the duration, intensity, and one-directionality of contact.

But with a novel, the reader performs all the characters on the stage of his imagination, using the stage directions provided by the narrator. Evidence of this performative element is the widely varying response of different readers to the same character. Tolkien is a good example: his Gandalf is a figure of power or a colossal bore; Samwise is a cringing servant or a sturdy companion. One senses that readers bringing back such disparate reports have "seen" different "productions" of the novel: in one case as clumsy as a school pageant, in another a rendering by the Royal Shakespeare Company. Curiously enough, it is often unsophisticated readers who mount the most vivid mental productions, while professional critics give half-hearted read-throughs.

This theatrical analogy, like the reference to prestidigitation in the last chapter, is intended to reflect the conventionality of narrative elements, especially the necessity of collusion between writer and reader. But it is dangerous to carry the analogy much further, for characters in narrative fiction are fundamentally different from theatrical characters. This difference is demonstrated most clearly in fantasy. In illustrating the unusual treatment of character by some fantasy writers, however, I hope also to suggest new and productive ways of analyzing the status of fictional characters in general.

To begin with, fantasy characters very rarely resemble the sort of beings found in Ibsen's plays or nineteenth-century social novels. Ursula K. Le Guin borrows Virginia Woolf's name for the latter sort of characters—Mrs. Brown ("Science Fiction and Mrs. Brown," *The Language of the Night* 101–19). Mrs. Brown is any fictional character who not only comes to life for the duration of the fiction but also continues to haunt the reader. She seems larger, if not than life, at least than the text in which she has her existence. She is usually based on close observation of real people—Woolf says she saw her Mrs. Brown for a few moments in a railway carriage. She represents, without generalizing, human nature; that is, we recognize in her (described) appearance, her (recounted) actions, and her (reported) words a being separate from but similar to ourselves. She can trigger a powerful affective response that goes something like, "If I were not myself, I might be this person. I know what it is to be Mrs. Brown." To this extent, Mrs. Brown is equivalent to the psychological concept of the Other, recognition of which is essential to the formation of the Self.

Le Guin's essay primarily concerns the presence or absence of Mrs. Brown in science fiction, but she deals briefly with fantasy as well:

> If any field of literature has no, can have no Mrs. Browns in it, it is fantasy—straight fantasy, the modern descendent of folktale, fairy tale, and myth. These genres deal with archetypes, not with characters. The very essence of Elfland is that Mrs. Brown can't get there—not unless she is changed, changed utterly, into an old mad witch, or a fair young princess, or a loathely Worm. (106–107)

Though she later qualifies this statement, Le Guin here identifies fantasy with a completely different conception of character, using the Jungian term *archetype*. Rather than basing characters primarily on observations of behavior, the writer of fantasy, she says, can "break the complex conscious daylight personality into its archetypal unconscious dreamtime components, Mrs. Brown becoming a princess, a toad, a worm, a witch, a child—so Tolkien in his wisdom broke Frodo into four: Frodo, Sam, Sméagol and Gollum; perhaps five, counting Bilbo" (107). In other words, the characters in a fairy tale or modern fantasy can be viewed as internal phenomena, embodiments of psychological phenomena acting out their struggle toward integration in a projected landscape of the mind. Another fantasy writer, Stephen Donaldson, propounds much the same Jungian conception of character and setting in his essay "Epic Fantasy in the Modern World." Both writers affirm the legitimacy of such a conception of character. It is not inartistic, as E. M. Forster and others have maintained, to have characters whose primary significance is their advancement of the story. Some psychological processes are inaccessible except through the narrative interaction of archetypal characters.

Having equated the novelistic character with the Other, then, we might put fantastic characters on the side of the Self, the inner, hidden Self that may have little to do with habits, mannerisms, and daily concerns. Yet there is a paradox here. What is the source of these archetypal characters? Do they arise from introspection and self-analysis? Are they intensely private symbolic systems, each encoding a unique psychic balance? Obviously not. Fantasy learned this conception of character from fairy tales and myths, which are by definition public property. Anonymous, traditional, their origins lost in pre-literate prehistory, magical fairy tales would seem to express the identity of the group, not the individual. Until such stories were collected and transcribed, their existence depended on continual re-creation through communal performance. In oral traditional societies, tale-telling is the principal means of inducting the individual into the worldview of the group.

The distinction of Self and Other, then, does not cover the difference between the two conceptions of character represented by fairy tales and novels, between Beauty and Mrs. Brown. Insofar as Beauty reflects a fundamental psychological principle, she relates to interior experience, but she is also a social phenomenon—the product of generations of public performance (adapted, in the form we know her, according to the literary tastes of eighteenth-century France and the artistry of Madame de Beaumont). Mrs. Brown is portrayed strictly through external details—Virginia Woolf describes her size, age, clothing, expression, actions, and speech— and yet is doubly expressive of inner life, her own and her observer's. In a sense, Beauty has no self, being so entirely at the service of the story that she does not even have a name, only a nickname designating her function. Mrs. Brown is all identity and no story; if Woolf had put her into a novel instead of an essay she would still refuse, as it were, to perform to order.

This last distinction suggests a way to describe the characters of folk narratives without making a priori assumptions about psychological or social function. They may be defined as essential elements of the narrative itself, called "functions" by Propp and the Russian Formalists. A character in a fairy tale *is* what he *does*. Beauty is only secondarily the pretty daughter of a merchant; she is primarily the one who redeems the Beast. Characters in other tales are similarly role-bound: hero, helper, giant-killer, adversary. Like novelistic characters, they are verbal constructs, assemblages of textual fragments, but unlike the characters of realistic fiction, they consist primarily of descriptions of movement and transformation. The textual clues that comprise a realistic character, as Seymour Chatman tells us, add up to a set of consistent (or believably inconsistent) traits, by which we could recognize the character even without a proper name to go by (119–25). The textual clues that comprise a fairy tale character add up to an achieved movement, like the testing of the hero or the rescue of a prisoner. Both kinds of character are forms of narrative discourse. Neither is inherently superior. There is no particular virtue in being motivated by envy, melancholy, or some other trait rather than by narrative necessity.

But modern fantasy is not simply a revival of the fairy tale, and its characters can combine the two forms of discourse, just as the genre of fantasy combines the mimetic and fantastic modes. Frodo performs the role of hero, but he fits into that role only approximately; in some ways he barely fills the outline, in others he is too solid to be contained within it. We know too much about Frodo. As Le Guin says, he "really looks very like Mrs. Brown, except that he has furry feet; a short, thin, tired-looking fellow, wearing a gold ring on a chain round his neck, and heading rather disconsolately eastward, on foot" (107). Like no other character in *LOTR*, Frodo establishes himself independently of his role in the story. We know his habits, likes, dislikes, kindness, occasional pettiness, courage, laziness: a whole set of novelistic traits, most of which will need to be pared away by the end of the narrative if he is to become the Hero it requires for resolution, a grander but simpler being than a mere hobbit.

Tolkien underscores Frodo's uncomfortable transformation from realistic character to story function with a few magical clues. A device that Tolkien uses frequently might be called the "seeming": the brief glimpse (occasionally false) of an underlying reality. An example of a seeming that reveals Frodo's new stature is Sam's vision of him with a temporarily cooperative Gollum:

> For a moment it appeared to Sam that his master had grown and Gollum had shrunk: a tall stern shadow, a mighty lord who hid his brightness in a grey cloud, and at his feet a little whining dog. (II, 225)

Tolkien's heroic figures are invariably tall and bright. Critics of his technique mistake these for character traits, whereas they are more properly role-markers.

Sam's seeming shows how Frodo is expanding to fit his destined role, but other glimpses show the cost. His individual character traits give way, marked in magical terms by a gradual fading. Gandalf first notices this change after Frodo is wounded by the Ringwraiths: "But to the wizard's eye there was a faint change, just a hint as it were of transparency, about him, and especially about the left hand that lay outside the coverlet" (I, 235).

Both transformations are essentially complete by the time Frodo reaches the gates of Mordor. As Sam sees him lying in the deathlike trance brought on by Shelob's poison, "Frodo's face was fair of hue again, pale but beautiful with an elvish beauty, as of one who has long passed the shadows" (II, 342). Frodo the hobbit is essentially dead; the elvish beauty and pallor (which are from one perspective the Hero's brightness, and from another the fading of individuality) mark his new identity. It should surprise no one that Frodo fails to fit into the life of the Shire after the return of the Fellowship. His proper milieu is no longer a setting but a story, and his story is over.

Modern fantasy thus draws on two traditions of characterization. To avoid confusion with psychological theories or value judgments, I will not call these character formulations *realistic* or *archetypal*. A. J. Greimas has provided a less loaded terminology: as an element in the construction of a story, a character may be called an *actant*—the French participial ending conveys the sense of *doing* that is essential to such characters. A character who is more interesting for his individual qualities than for his place in a shaped narrative is an *acteur* (Scholes, *Structuralism* 103), or, substituting the English form, an *actor*.

Fantasy, then, makes use of the narrative and semiotic code we call magic to examine the relationship between character as imitated person and character as story function, between actor and actant. One way it does so is by calling into question the continuity of traits by which the reader is accustomed to identify characters. A minor example is Tolkien's changing of Gandalf's identifying color from grey to white. Even so small a change causes confusion, for color was the primary external difference between Gandalf the Grey and Saruman the White. Other characters alter: Merry and Pippin grow taller (for which we are intended to read: more heroic) after drinking Treebeard's draughts. Frodo grows simultaneously grander and more wraithlike. Gollum shifts back and forth between beast and wizened hobbit. But within *LOTR,* for the most part, we are clearly alerted to the moments of change, and so the continuity of traits is at least partially preserved.

In other fantasies, however, characters are fed through the mechanism of magic like grapes through a wine press, emerging with unrecognizable shapes and flavors. Virtually any character trait can be altered magically: appearance, age, voice, emotional state, memory. In Patricia McKillip's Riddle-Master trilogy (1976–79), for instance, the hero Morgon learns to change his form to that of a tree:

> The chill from his motionlessness began to trouble him, then passed as the silence became a tangible thing measuring his breath, his heartbeat, seeping into his thoughts, his bones, until he felt hollowed, a shell of winter stillness. The trees circling him seemed to enclose a warmth like the stone houses at Kyrth, against the winter. Listening, he heard suddenly the hum of their veins, drawing life from deep beneath the snow, beneath the hard earth. He felt himself rooted, locked into the rhythms of the mountain; his own rhythms drained away from him, lost beyond memory in the silence that shaped him. (*The Riddle-Master of Hed* 184)

This tree does not share Morgon's appearance, his humanity, even his perceptions, yet the narrative demands that we accept it as Morgon. When, then, might the character be said to change identity? If the transformation were irreversible? If Morgon remained in tree form long enough to lose his memories of humanity? If we found out that he had originally been a tree, and that his human shape was an illusion? If another character came along claiming to be the real Morgon, with Morgon's memories to prove it? A fantasy can pose any of these questions simply by positing magical operations such as shape shifting, transfer of personalities, or reduplication of characters.

In the case of Morgon, although his identity passes intact through the tree episode, it undergoes more serious alteration as the narrative proceeds. Like Frodo, he is required to be a hero. The hero he must become already has a name: Star-Bearer. The stars are on his face, birthmarks, but they also appear on a harp and a sword made long before his birth: in other words, the identity predates the man. McKillip poses the dilemma in the form of a riddle, and riddles are, in her created world, the foundation of magic.

Other riddles emerge from the story to interact with Morgon's quest for his own identity. McKillip offers a set of names to be sorted out: names from ancient history, from cosmology, and from Morgon's personal experience. The High King, the High King's harpist, the Founder of Lungold, the Wizard Ghisteslwchlohm, the Riddle-Master Ohm, the Wizard Yrth (pun undoubtedly intended), the man called Deth (another serious pun), Earth-Master, Shape-Changer: all these identities are combined and recombined—ultimately into only two beings—as Morgon learns more about the past and present. Each reshuffling of the names of these others contributes also to his own self-definition.

McKillip's most unusual variation on the formation of character is to make the mimetic side, the actor, rather simple, and the story-function side, the actant, both complex and variable. Morgon's character is sketched briefly at the beginning, chiefly in terms of his youth, his intelligence, and his ties to his rural homeland. We are given just enough information to establish him as a believable type, not a memorable individual, before the story carries him away to begin his transformations. In the course of three volumes, he is called on to play a great many roles, so that we see him as questor, questioner, answerer, accuser, victim, bystander, lover, pratfaller, rescuer, and mystery. Each role calls on unforeseen abilities, which must then be integrated into the character as we have come to know him.

The entire story hinges on the interaction of power and identity, which are represented as contraries, like movement and structure or sea and land. Morgon ultimately must resolve the paradox, mastering both, becoming a self that is both Morgon and Star-Bearer, both person and story.

McKillip's technique of characterization illustrates fantasy's ability to bring two forms of discourse together in an irreducible and yet inseparable whole. To borrow a term from Mikhail Bakhtin, a fantasy character is essentially a dialogue. Mimesis speaks; story responds; character forms in the tension between the two (Todorov, *Mikhail Bakhtin* 60–63).

In both Tolkien's and McKillip's formulations of the dialogue, the discourse of the actor is introduced first, but that need not always be the case. Diana Wynne Jones begins *The Time of the Ghost* (1984) with the perceptions of a character who has virtually no realistic character traits, though neither the character nor the reader is at first aware of her undefined state. She is a ghost, of sorts, a disembodied consciousness with a memory of belonging in a particular place but no memory of who she is or was. She is also a plot device, as most fictional ghosts are: a need, to be fulfilled through the action of other characters.

Her need is to find out whose ghost she might be and how she got that way, but the question is not a simple one. As she accumulates experiences, she recovers partial memory and identity, but only to the point of being certain that she is one of four sisters, all of whom seem to be carrying on perfectly normal existences apart from herself.

The ghost faces a problem very like that confronted by a reader trying to get to know a character: how to assemble clues of various sorts—bits of conversation, random memories, relationships with other characters—into a coherent personality. Only in this case, her very existence depends on her ability to construct a self from the clues.

She begins by accepting the testimony of others. Though she is invisible, people sense her presence and sometimes speak to her before looking around to see nobody there:

Under the frown, Phyllis said wearily, "Your father's told you, I've told you. How many times have you been told to stay behind the green door, Sally?"

Warmth and comfort and pleasure swelled, as huge and swift as the balloon of panic had swelled earlier. Mother had seen her. Mother knew her. Mother knew who she was. She was Sally. Of course she was Sally. Everything was all right, even though she had gone and done an awful thing and interrupted Father while he was teaching. . . . Sally—yes, she was sure she was Sally—stood guiltily by the green door, wondering how to explain, as Phyllis turned her blue eyes and tired frown towards her. (11)

This, of course, is no solution, and Jones tells us so indirectly. Phyllis does not see her: retreat to Mother is impossible, despite the ghost's adoption of a childlike attitude, represented in the syntax of her thoughts. Nor do the multiple repetitions of the name guarantee its applicability to herself. In order to identify herself, to turn from actant into actor, she needs to do more than be named by a parent.

Her next step is self-justification. Having convinced herself she is Sally, she overhears the other three sisters criticizing her and silently argues with them:

I'm not like that! I'm not hysterical and I don't go on about my career. I'm not like Imogen. They're just seeing their own faults in me! And I don't grumble and criticise. I'm ever so meek and lowly really—sort of gentle and dazed and puzzled about life. (24)

Real progress begins only as she observes the other girls and starts to identify with them each in turn: "Sally found herself saying, *Imogen really is terribly unhappy!* Imogen's face, with its strong angel features, was somehow bloated from behind, with tears she was waiting to cry" (52). Then she comes into contact with the living Sally and is startled to find no identification:

She knew the girl was Sally. There had been no mistake there. Yet she had no sense of identity with her. She had no idea what this Sally thought and felt. She seemed just someone else she was forced to hover and watch, as she had watched Sally's sisters. (87)

The ghost can only hover and watch because the life of Sally and her sisters belongs to a different kind of narrative from her own. Her own story, surprisingly, concerns an old, cruel goddess, roused inadvertently and allayed only through sacrifice. Theirs, on the other hand, is a thoroughly believable story of squabbles and loyalty among four gifted but neglected sisters and their few allies among the male pupils at their parents' school. Ghost and goddess are pure narrative function; sisters and school are portraiture, with very little narrative movement.

Jones takes these two forms of discourse and forces them to mingle. The appearance of the ghost forces a change in the girls' condition, pushing them into the realm of story, where happier endings are possible. The ghost's observation of herself and her sisters (from a vantage point seven years in the future, it turns out) gives way to interaction with them. She absorbs a measure of their solidity (on a literal as well as figurative level, in a scene in which the girls reenact Odysseus's adventure with the shades), and their help wins her freedom from the goddess.

Kept quietly in the background throughout is a metaphoric level, in which spectral existence represents the character's actual self-effacement. One can see the ghost as a role-bound woman: the unnoticed observer, powerless, able to act only by influencing those around her, condemned always to follow the movements of others. That is, as Jones hints, the life the character has been leading for the seven years between the time of the haunting and the time she discovers is actually her present moment. Thus, her immersion in a story-role represents no great loss of personality; instead, the interplay between the two types of characterization allows her to break free of societal limitations and, for the first time, become a three-dimensional character.

The structure of *Time of the Ghost* can help clarify the puzzling relationship of character to such concepts as Self and Other or individual and group. The ghost character's main claim to selfhood is her ability to report to herself on what she is perceiving and doing. Julian Jaynes, in his problematic but fascinating *The Origin of Consciousness in the Breakdown of the Bicameral Mind* (1976), suggests that such an act of "narratizing" constitutes what we call consciousness:

> consciousness is an operation rather than a thing, a repository, or a function. It operates by way of analogy, by way of constructing an analog space with an analog "I" that can observe that space, and move metaphorically in it. It operates on any reactivity, excerpts relevant aspects, narratizes and conciliates them together in a metaphorical space where such meanings can be manipulated like things in space. (65–66)

The ghost is such an analog "I," and the entire narrative is essentially the story she tells herself. This is represented stylistically by using for the narrative voice what is called indirect free discourse, or quotation of her thoughts grammatically converted into third person, with occasional direct access marked by italics:

> She could not even feel anything from the clump of nettles she seemed to
> be standing in. *Seemed is the right word,* she thought unhappily. *Let's
> face it. I'm not just invisible. I haven't got a body at all.* (7)

The implied narrator of all this—a woman lying in a hospital bed
seven years hence—is projecting a self, a consciousness, into a fictional
space that is, nevertheless, real, thanks to the magic. She is delving into
memory to construct a story that will, as Jaynes says only stories can do,
conciliate the contradictions of her life, past and present:

> If I ask you to think of a mountain meadow and a tower at the same time,
> you automatically conciliate them by having the tower rising from the
> meadow. But if I ask you to think of the mountain meadow and an ocean
> at the same time, conciliation tends not to occur and you are likely to
> think of one and then the other. You can only bring them together by a
> narratization. (Jaynes 65)

The only analog the ghost can construct to represent herself is a
bodiless, memoryless intelligence—that is one of the conflicts she must
narrate into resolution. Her projected self lacks a surface with which to
interact with the world: it is an inside with no outside. Yet she does not
exist in complete isolation. She is in contact with the common property of
humanity: language, the ability to narrate, and archetypal motifs such as
ghost and *goddess*. She illustrates the paradox discussed earlier: what is
most completely representative of the individual psyche is also most
traditional.

The other characters, though, including her past self, are most recognizable in their interactions with one another and their environment.
They exist at the boundary of the Self and the Other. This is where
physical appearance and gestures occur and where they are noted, where
language manifests itself as communication or misunderstanding, and
where the caress or the slap translates the impulses of the Self into
demonstrations of emotion.

Without boundaries, there is no distinction between the Self and
primordial Humanity. In Jones's terms, the ghost has no way to hide from
the goddess until she learns to draw the magic circle of identity around
her Self, and that circle, that identity, is the product of confrontation with
a community of others. It is their boundary as well as hers; like a bubble in
a froth, each character is defined by the thin membranes that both join it
to and separate it from its fellows. These are the complementary conceptions of character from which Jones has constructed her story. Speaking first separately and then in dialogue, the two modes of discourse come
together to create a character linked with both fantasy and mimesis.

Alan Garner's characters also begin as pure actants, but in order to trace their evolution into a more dialogic conception, we must follow Garner's own development as a writer from *The Weirdstone of Brisingamen* (1960) to *The Owl Service* (1967).

Garner's early novels, *The Weirdstone of Brisingamen* and *The Moon of Gomrath* (1963), both tell of the waking of ancient magic in the contemporary countryside of Cheshire, Garner's home region. In both books, two children named Colin and Susan act as the focus for the magic and the narrative itself. Around them, wizards, dwarfs, and various other figures from English legend struggle and plot for mastery. These supernatural characters are divided into teams—good and evil—but there is little sense of what distinguishes the two sides, for neither plays entirely fair. The wizard Cadellin is no less willing to use the children as pawns than is his evil counterpart (and near twin) Grimnir.

In *The Weirdstone,* which Garner later called "a fairly bad book" ("A Bit More Practice" 197), all the conventional characters are either caricatures or blanks. The country people of Alderly Edge, like farmer Gowther Mossock, speak in thick dialect, they are repositories of ancient stories, and they are sturdy and stolid. That is about the extent of their characterization. The children speak in a colorless standard English, and then only to comment on the action of the story, as if they had no past, no interests, no emotions outside of the action going on around them. There is a vacuum where the discourse of the actor should be.

The magical characters, on the other hand, are drawn in simple, bold strokes. The Morrigan, for instance, a witch and shape shifter, is the first character to warrant a physical description, and Garner's description immediately establishes her as a force in the action:

> She looked about forty-five years old, was powerfully built ("fat" was the word Susan used to describe her), and her head rested firmly on her shoulders without appearing to have much of a neck at all. Two deep lines ran from either side of her nose to the corners of her wide, thin-lipped mouth, and her eyes were rather too small for her broad head. Strangely enough her legs were thin and spindly, so that in outline she resembled a well-fed sparrow. . . . (13)

We recognize this character, not so much as a realistic portrai·, but as a sort of velocity, like an arrow drawn on a map to show the direction of traffic. The story is going to go in a certain direction, and the Morrigan is going to push it there. Each of the magical beings the children meet is a similar vector marker, and the outcome of the story is their sum.

The most striking characters in the book are those who are most completely at the service of story. Cadellin, whose long conversations with the children push him toward actor status, is a rather stiff and conventional rendering of the wizard archetype. In contrast, beings whose purely functional nature is represented by their being given titles rather than names—the Morrigan, the Mara—are often vividly original. Likewise, the clumsiness that characterizes Garner's use of actorial discourse disappears when he describes movement and magic, the discourse of the actant.

In *The Moon of Gomrath,* Garner consolidates his strengths, the visualization of fantastic scenes and beings and the economical description of action, while at the same time beginning to amend his weaknesses. In this second book, Susan and Colin are no longer interchangeable, nor do they remain unaffected by the action around them, which is itself more coherently conceived.

In contrast with *The Weirdstone*'s plots and counterplots for possession of an amulet in which the audience has very little interest—a Hitchcockian McGuffin—*The Moon of Gomrath* has a single main sequence of action that continually rises in intensity. This means that the actants, as well as the actors, are used more effectively, for their respective directional pushes add up to a shapelier story.

In that story, actor and actant begin to work together in dialogue fashion, for Susan and, to a lesser extent, Colin find themselves altered this time around, as they were not in their previous contact with magic. The action begins by picking up a loose thread from the prior story: Susan has had to give up her heirloom bracelet, and in exchange the Lady of the Lake has given her a silver band with unreadable markings—the Mark of Fohla. It is, not surprisingly, a thing of power, and Susan is asked to lend it. Wearing it has marked her, however, and its loss makes her vulnerable to attack, which comes in the form of a legendary beast, the Brollachan. In horse form, this creature tempts Susan to ride and carries her off into the depths of a lake. She returns with wet and weedy hair and a hand that feels like a hoof: she is possessed.

The pattern is repeated: the solution to one problem leads to a new danger, each time plunging the children deeper into the world of magic. The return of the bracelet to Susan's wrist casts out the Brollachan, but sends her spirit to the realm of the Daughters of the Moon, who wear bracelets like hers and who greet her as a sister. Her body, meanwhile, lies in a coma. Colin brings her back by gathering a magic flower by moonlight, but in doing so wakes the Wild Hunt. None of this makes Cadellin happy, for the powers that are being roused are Old Magic, indivisible into good and evil, rather than his own intellectual High Magic. He describes what has happened to Susan since she put on the bracelet:

"She was saved, and is protected, only by the Mark of Fohla—her blessing and her curse. For it guards her against the evil that would crush her, and it leads her ever further from the ways of human life." (56)

Susan does not share his apprehensions: she is eager to learn the powers that come with her bracelet. In the end, she rides with the Wild Hunt and the Daughters of the Moon to put the Brollachan to flight, and would be happy to ride off into legend with them. Her time, though, has not yet come:

But as they crossed the valley, one of the riders dropped behind, and Colin saw that it was Susan. She lost ground, though her speed was no less, and the light that formed her died, and in its place was a smaller, solid figure that halted, forlorn, in the white wake of the riding. (138–39)

With this curious sour note in an otherwise happy ending, Garner found a theme that he developed further in *Elidor* (1965) and *The Owl Service*. In the former, four children pass from a derelict church in a Manchester slum into an enchanted land where they are hailed as prophesied saviors. A successful quest seems to validate the prophecy, but its accomplishment only takes a quarter of the book. The remaining and more interesting portion concerns their return home, and the strains of incorporating the memory of glory into their mundane suburban lives and of being heroes in an unheroic age. The dialogue between actor and actant grows more poignant when the character is aware of his dialogic nature, and that is one key to the success of *Elidor* and the greater success of Garner's next story.

Made up largely of conversation, tightly restricted in setting, and compressed in time, *The Owl Service* resembles a play. By the time he wrote this novel, Garner had mastered the art of making characters reveal themselves through speech, gesture, and the other elements of the discourse of the actor. He credits his new facility to a stint of interviewing for radio and television:

This often meant having to condense what somebody spent an hour saying into three minutes—without cheating!—preserving the root of what they were trying to say. The pressure of this programming meant having to listen very very carefully to what was being said. (Wintle and Fisher 230)

Garner throws his interviewing skills into generating believable, sharply individuated, and highly compressed dialogue for his three chief characters: Gwyn, Alison, and Roger. Less fully explored but equally vivid are Gwyn's mother Nancy, Roger's father Clive, and even Alison's mother Margaret, who is never on stage but who dominates the lives of the others. Unlike Garner's earlier heroes, who seemed to have no ties outside of the story, Gwyn and the others represent the intersection of a large number of conflicting loyalties. Gwyn is bright, ambitious, poor, illegitimate, and Welsh. Roger's mother abandoned him and his nouveau riche, ex-Army father. His father has married Alison's mother, so they are step-siblings trying not to dislike one another. Alison represents old money and is, like Roger, English. These factors throw up barriers to the communication all three desperately need to establish, especially after they find themselves caught up as actants in an ancient story.

Whereas Garner's earlier story lines were cobbled together from multiple sources—local legend, Scandinavian myth, fairy tale—*The Owl Service* draws on a single source which is explicitly acknowledged in the text. It is the tale of Lleu Llaw Gyffes, from the *Mabinogion*. Lleu, whose mother has cursed him so that he can marry neither mortal woman nor goddess, is given a bride made of flowers by the wizard Gwydion. The beautiful Blodeuwedd, though, betrays her husband with a neighbor, Gronw Pebyr, and with him she plots Lleu's death. Rescued by Gwydion, Lleu kills Gronw, and Blodeuwedd is transformed into an owl. Their story of love, betrayal, murder, and metamorphosis impinges on the present-day narrative when Alison finds a set of plates, the owl service of the title, with a floral design that can be rearranged to form owl faces.

The characters live in the same Welsh valley where Blodeuwedd was created and punished. The forces that came together to produce tragic legend still exist within this small community, in the flowers from which Blodeuwedd was formed—oak, broom, and meadowsweet—and the passions that undid her. Dammed up like a mountain stream, these forces periodically seek outlet. In every generation, three victims take on the roles of husband, wife, and lover. A generation ago, the actants were Huw, the half-mad gardener and hereditary lord of the valley; Gwyn's mother Nancy; and Bertram, the cousin from whom Alison's father inherited the estate. Now the roles have shifted, with Huw standing as Gwydion to Gwyn's Lleu and Nancy as Lleu's vengeful mother, who in the original legend denies him name, armor, and a bride until tricked by Gwydion.

So we have three unremarkable teenagers reenacting a love story of heroic proportions, like that of Tristan and Isolde or Arthur and Guinevere. The distance between actor and actant is enormous, seemingly unbridgeable, and yet Garner convinces us that such an overlay is a valid formulation of character. Huw, Alison, and Roger are capable of enacting the narrative functions known as Lleu, Blodeuwedd, and Gronw: furthermore, they know they are doing so, know the tragic outcome implied, and are seeking, with all the resources available to them as actors, to prevent the cycle from taking its accustomed course.

They do not have all this knowledge at the beginning, of course. All they are aware of is that something strange is happening. The magic seems at first to be external to themselves: scrabbling noises in the attic that lead them to the flowered plates, Alison's tracings of the owl pattern that keep disappearing, a plaster wall that crumbles away spontaneously to reveal a portrait. The twin motifs of owls and flowers recur in every case: the woman in the portrait stands against a background of clover; the clover heads are made of claws.

Beauty and half-understood sexual desire alternate with violence, as when Roger is bathing in the stream where Lleu's spear struck Gronw. The scene is almost sybaritic at first:

> Roger splashed through the shallows to the bank. A slab of rock stood out of the ground close by him, and he sprawled backwards into the foam of meadowsweet that grew thickly round its base. He gathered the stems in his arms and pulled the milky heads down over his face to shield him from the sun. (13)

But Roger's dalliance turns surreal when the spear thrown by Lleu centuries before again pierces the stone behind which Gronw once hid:

> Something flew by him, a blink of dark on the leaves. It was heavy, and fast, and struck hard. He felt the vibration through the rock, and he heard a scream.
>
> Roger was on his feet, crouching, hands wide, but the meadow was empty, and the scream was gone: he caught its echo in the farmer's distant voice and a curlew away on the mountain. There was no one in sight; his heart raced, and he was cold in the heat of the sun. He looked at his hands. The meadowsweet had cut him, lining his palm with red beads. The flowers stank of goat. (13–14)

Such incidents supply pieces to the puzzle while helping to convince the protagonists that the puzzle is no mere intellectual game. Other clues come from Huw, whose madness makes more and more sense—whose Welsh-influenced verb forms, even, help convey the sense of the past impinging on the present:

> "There is a man being killed at that place," said Huw: "old time."
> "Was there now!"
> "Yes," said Huw. "He has been taking the other man's wife." (33–34)

To Huw and the other local residents, there is no question that myth is a matter of here and now. The outsiders Alison and Roger, though, and even Gwyn, cut off from local culture by his schooling, have a hard time believing that their lives are being warped into a pattern they think of as a quaint piece of local color. Though they find the text of the legend in a book borrowed from Gwyn's English teacher, it is not until each of them experiences firsthand the emotions that led to the original tragedy that they begin to have any real understanding of its significance. They learn to think of it, as Huw does, in the present tense.

The supernatural events that occur in the course of the book are dramatic but inconclusive. There are no sudden transformations, no glowing jewels, no monsters. Alison's paper owls disappear and are found surrounding a stuffed owl in the shed. Her anger shreds a book and sends its fragments swarming through the air at Gwyn. Gwyn is led through the woods by a will-o'-the-wisp and sees a figure that is not Alison: "The figure was still there at the end of the causeway, waiting, under the tree, head and shoulders, and arms and the slim body, and then he saw, no less clearly, leaves, and branches, thicket and moonlight, and no one waiting" (67). Roger takes a photograph through the hole in the stone of Gronw and it shows, blurrily, a horseman raising a spear. These events are markers of interior changes in the three main characters, glimpses of a kind of experience that cannot be told through the discourse of the actor, though the outward signs can be shown.

Garner takes the dialogic nature of character about as far as it can be taken; the book's every scene advances both conceptions at once. It takes at least two readings to sort them out, particularly in the early scenes before all the clues are given. Oftentimes the same descriptive phrase or line of speech will function on both levels. The setting itself reflects the double nature of the characters. The house is a society in miniature, while the valley provides the raw materials for myth: water and weather, flowers and feathers, mating and dying. Human beings live in both worlds, though some are blind to the latter or excluded from the former.

As the two forms of existence—actors and actants—draw together, the natural world imposes its presence more strongly. In the final scene, the house fills with feathers:

> They circled and clung: circled and clung: the owl dance he had found in the dust. They were moving on the ceiling and the walls, and he began to see the patterns that had followed Huw in the rain: eyes and wings and sharpness: winged eyes, yellow, and blackness curved: all in the rafters and the wall and the feathers everywhere. (154)

At the same time, the social reality feeds the magic, because it is keyed to the three protagonists who have been chosen to reenact the story: " 'She is coming, and will use what she finds, and you have only hate in you,' said Huw. 'Always and always and always' " (155). "She" is Blodeuwedd, not just a woman in a story, but a goddess of beauty and cruelty, embodied in the natural objects of the valley and in the passions of humans. The beauty comes from nature; the cruelty from the admixture of humanity.

As Garner uses the two forms of characterization, each expands upon the other. The realistic characters of Gwyn, Alison, and Roger make the reenactment of the legend possible; the legend gives them grandeur. The legend says that Gwyn is not merely a bright, shy, unhappy teenager, but also the wronged lord of his Welsh kingdom. It says that Blodeuwedd is invoked whenever a young girl blooms into womanhood and that she turns dangerous when locked up against her will in someone else's life. Huw, who has already lived through his own cycle, has gained an understanding of the Blodeuwedd within his Nancy:

> She was made for her lord. Nobody is asking her if she wants him. It is bitter twisting to be shut up with a person you are not liking very much. I think she is often longing for the time when she was flowers on the mountain, and it is making her cruel, as the rose is growing thorns. (55)

The structure of Garner's book suggests that no character is complete until she has encountered her own mythic narrative: the discourse of Mrs. Brown, by which we usually identify ourselves as well as those we meet, lacks depth and direction without the discourse of Beauty or Blodeuwedd. Yet the latter discourse is dangerous, leading to death or madness as easily as to a happy ending. Of the three primary characters in *The Owl Service*, Alison is too unformed and Gwyn too deeply wounded to work their way through the myth to a resolution. Roger, the least sympathetic through most of the action, proves to be the one able to learn from his role and thus to divert the story from its apparently inevitable end. Something in his ordinary past experience enables him to take hold of the power of the myth, and, as Huw says, "leash it, yet set it free . . . so that no one else may suffer" (135).

The Owl Service suggests that the number of ways the discourse of actants can interact with that of actors is limitless, that each combination will result in a different formulation. When Huw becomes Llew Llaw Gyffes, the result is not the same as when he later plays the part of Gwydion. Gwyn's version of Llew is something else again. Yet in each case, the pattern that emerges from the dialogue illuminates both elements. The archetypal role may end up effacing the actor or disappearing under the weight of the actor's traits, or the two may strike a balance, as Patricia McKillip's Star-Bearer does. No matter what the result, an important component has been restored to the concept of character.

In the stories that combine literary greatness with popular appeal, from the *Odyssey* to *Great Expectations,* characters are both determiners of and subservient to the action. The pleasure is in seeing believable analogs of humanity acting out the patterns of fairy tale or myth. The more realistic the discourse of the actor, the more strongly we identify with his shock or pleasure at finding himself transformed into actant. Fiction that arbitrarily foregoes the possibility of such transformation—fiction with no heroes, helpers, or villains—gains verisimilitude at the expense of psychological and philosophical range.

These fantasies echo the old and recently rediscovered truth that only through such narrative structures can we define ourselves and our relationships with others. From our first "memories," which are not infrequently constructed from anecdotes told to us by family members (Baldwin), to the narrative constructions through which the psychoanalytic subject presents himself to the analyst or the testifying churchgoer to God, we examine our experiences and our characters by dropping them into the stream of a story and seeing where they wash ashore. Writers of fantasy reflect this process when they set up the dialogue of actor and actant. Its mixed parentage—fairy tale on the mother's side, realistic fiction on the father's—gives fantasy a unique ability to investigate the twofold process of constructing a self.

SIX

Women's Coming of Age in Fantasy

A STRENGTH AND A WEAKNESS of fantasy is its reliance on traditional storytelling forms and motifs. By making its conventional basis explicit and primary, rather than submerging traditional tale types or character functions beneath a surface of apparent reported reality, fantasy is empowered to reimagine both character and story, as we have seen. But a willingness to return to the narrative structures of the past can entail as well an unquestioning acceptance of its social structures.

This danger is particularly evident when the inherited story focuses on the process of coming of age, the transition from immature individual to mature member of society. In the societies from which we derive our legacy of myths and fairy tales, coming of age was a process of accommodating oneself to a strictly defined social role: hunter, chieftain, farmer, king. The passage from childhood to adult status was generally marked by the enactment of rituals which not only marked the individual's transition but also at the same time reaffirmed the hierarchical order in which the newly adult member was to find a place. Sometimes accompanying the rituals and sometimes serving in their place were spoken narratives. These told of a young hero's displacement, transformation, and return—the fundamental pattern of both the hero monomyth, as described by Joseph Campbell, and of the fairy tale, as analyzed by Vladimir Propp.

We see this pattern reproduced in some form in virtually every modern fantasy. For example, in Lloyd Alexander's Chronicles of Prydain (1964–68) an orphaned young man discovers a destiny, true love, and his identity. T. H. White's *The Sword in the Stone* (1938) describes the transformation of the child Wart into King Arthur. The title character of Le Guin's *A Wizard of Earthsea* (1968) matures by testing his powers and learning his own limits. Tolkien describes the way an amiable young hobbit grows into a heroic and somber figure. George MacDonald's *Phantastes* (1858) concerns a youth who wakes up in a room transformed into woodland and undergoes a series of tests and adventures that lead him to self-knowledge. Each of these coming-of-age stories reflects traditional sources, such as the tale-type known as the "sorcerer's apprentice," on which the second example is partially modeled. From the earliest traditional fairy tales to the most recent fantasy novels, protagonists have moved from the end of childhood (or at least a condition of unformedness) to adulthood as the story unfolds. The magical adventures are tied together and the story given shape by the hero's gradual assumption of his proper powers and his place in society.

Each of the protagonists referred to above—Taran Wanderer, Wart, Ged, Frodo, and Anodos—is male. That's not surprising; a majority of the central figures in fiction are male, reflecting cultural biases and the prevalence of men in the ranks of writers. But the creator of one of those characters is a woman. The treatment of the coming-of-age story by women writers such as Ursula K. Le Guin demonstrates how a tradition may be made to reflect contemporary concerns, and how inherited story structures may be used to question the practices and beliefs that gave rise to them.

Le Guin chose the young man Ged as the hero of her first major fantasy *A Wizard of Earthsea*. Not until the second book of her trilogy, *The Tombs of Atuan* (1971), did she explore directly the coming of age of a young woman. The experience of that character, Arha, is significantly different from that of Ged, whom we may take as typical of the male hero. Ged begins in obscurity but soon attracts attention for his native gifts in sorcery, leaves the domestic world of his aunt's house, undergoes an apprenticeship under a (male) master who gives him a new name, attends a school for wizards (all male), disobeys an injunction, wanders the world looking for a cure for the evil he has unleashed, is tempted by a (female) witch, bests a dragon in a test of wits, and finally overcomes the evil. Ambitious, proud, and impulsive, he must learn the limits of his powers. His only real adversary is himself, and his chief accomplishment is self-mastery.

For Arha, however, the problem is unleashing rather than mastering herself, and outside rather than within the institutional constraints of her culture. Accordingly, for Le Guin the problem is to find a way of adapting the conventions of fantasy to reflect this other kind of coming of age. Her solution, drawing upon her knowledge of earlier narratives and of anthropological studies of rites of passage, is to create a new assemblage, with new meanings, out of existing materials. Other women writers in turn have learned from her techniques. Like the women's art of quilting, fantasy writing is a cooperative enterprise, in which individual vision is expressed within prescribed forms, and innovation is an outgrowth of the process of continuity.

A large proportion of contemporary fantasy fiction is written by women. Patricia McKillip, Diana Wynne Jones, Susan Cooper, R. A. MacAvoy, and dozens of other writers have found fantasy—with its conventions derived from fairy tale, romance, supernatural legend, and myth—to be an appropriate vehicle for conveying the ideas and experiences they have found significant enough to work into narrative form. These writers and the women who explored the mode of fantasy before them constitute a tradition of a new sort. Thelma Shinn's *Worlds within Women* (1986) and Charlotte Spivack's *Merlin's Daughters* (1987) both describe the thematic consistency within contemporary fantastic literature by women: drawing on common experiences and knowledge of one another's work, women fantasists are engaged in such joint enterprises as refurbishing the archetypal images of the goddess, redefining the qualities of heroism to include female experience, and reaffirming women's access to the narrative storehouse of the past.

Shinn suggests that the marginal status of the fantastic within our culture makes it analogous to earlier orally transmitted materials of myth: "these ephemeral publications which go out of print quickly and into imaginative retellings easily are as close to an oral tradition as can be found in the larger contemporary society" (189–90). Within a popular art form such as fantasy, even non-formulaic works play off one another, borrowing freely and following up implications from earlier texts. In this way, the body of modern fantasy—and this is true of fantasy by men as well—comes to resemble a mythology: that is, a compilation of narratives that expresses a society's conception of itself, its individual members, and their place in the universe.

Coming of age is central in any mythology. Like all rites of passage or of initiation, it marks the passage of an individual from one state to another: from one tribe to another, from the laity to the priesthood, from life to death, or, in this case, from childhood to adulthood and full participation in society. Arnold van Gennep, whose 1908 study of *Les rites de passage* stands behind most popular treatments of the subject and thus shapes the way we continue to think of it, treats these rites as essentially concerned with changes of status in males:

> Transitions from group to group and from one social situation to the next are looked on as implicit in the very fact of existence, so that a man's life comes to be made up of a succession of stages with similar ends and beginnings: birth, social puberty, marriage, fatherhood, advancement to a higher class, occupational specialization, and death. (3)

This one-sided emphasis on "a man's life," ignoring a woman's, probably reflects both van Gennep's own bias and that of the cultures he is examining. Until recently, few ethnologists would have thought to look for women's rituals, and unless fieldworkers were themselves women, much of women's culture was inaccessible to them. Van Gennep's study primarily documents male activities from birth to grave, discussing women only in conjunction with pregnancy, childbirth, and marriage, and the last with respect to the man's acquisition of a wife. Mircea Eliade, in his *Rites and Symbols of Initiation* (1958), has more to say about female initiation, but he points out that such rituals typically lack the element of spiritual revelation present in the puberty rites of boys, being more concerned with marking the onset of menstruation and other such physical changes (47).

Do women come of age? In van Gennep's view perhaps not, for he considers women and children to form a single social group. Boys require a drastic break from this group to that of adult men; girls merely work their way through it. The further implication is that women never do become fully adult, that they are like those salamanders that stay underwater all their lives, able to reproduce but otherwise still in the gill-breathing, immature stage.

More recent studies, such as those summarized in Bruce Lincoln's *Emerging from the Chrysalis* (1981), suggest that women's initiation rites may actually outnumber men's (Lincoln 3), but that the nature of those rites is different enough from the anthropologist's conceptual model to have been dismissed as trivial or nonexistent. Van Gennep hypothesized a three-step process as basic to all rites of passage: separation of the candidate from the community, a period of ordeals and instruction, and reincorporation into the community under a new identity (Lincoln 100). In women's rituals, however, "something different seems to be at work, and in place of van Gennep's terms I would suggest three others: enclosure, metamorphosis (or magnification), and emergence" (Lincoln 101). Characteristically, the adolescent girl is secluded within her own home, often in an inner room, at or before her first menstruation. There she is considered to take on the identity of a culture heroine or goddess, like the Navajo Changing Woman (Lincoln 24); often the incarnation is marked by special costume. When she emerges into society, she renews the gifts of fertility and order originally brought by the mythic figure she represents.

But such rituals are not widely known; some are not even recognized by the societies in which they occur as equivalent to male initiations (Lincoln 35). Thus the belief that they do not exist continues to prevail even in scholarly circles. Carolyn Heilbrun reflects the general view when she suggests that women even in our own culture have no coming-of-age ritual and that they pay a psychological penalty for the lack:

All societies, from the earliest and most primitive to today's, have cere- moniously taken the boy from the female domain and urged his identity as a male, as a responsible unfeminine individual, upon him. The girl under- goes no such ceremony, but she pays for serenity of passage with a lack of selfhood and of the will to autonomy that only the struggle for identity can confer. (104)

A fantasy writer can invent a ritual for herself, holding her own imaginative initiation ceremony. But she faces limitations not faced by her male counterparts. If she is aware of the female rites of passage that do exist, she may not be content to induct her characters into the female roles to which those rites lead. The challenge she faces is to retain the values of the female initiation—its bestowal of identity and mystery upon the initiand—without turning her characters into tribal mothers and drudges. To do so, she must turn to other models from life and literature.

However, such models have long been difficult to find, especially in print. Copying the male initiation story with a female protagonist is one solution, but an inadequate one if the writer wishes to connect with women's actual experience in our culture. Few women even today can find in their own lives any analog of the male hero's freedom of movement or his expectation of power and rank at the end of his quest. An effective female initiation fantasy should be, at least at the beginning, more recog- nizably grounded in the biological and social reality of a woman's life, but in the course of events it should somehow transcend that reality.

The mainstream novel of the eighteenth and nineteenth centuries mirrors social realities, but it has no mechanism for transcending them. For this reason, it has little to offer women in the way of successful transitions to maturity. Beginning with Samuel Richardson's influential creations, youthful women in such novels are generally confined to two fates. They marry, like Pamela, or die, like Clarissa. Either fate ends the heroine's development.

One should note that this limitation applies only to stories of young women: there is a large class of fiction that "shows women developing later in life, after conventional expectations of marriage and motherhood have been fulfilled and found insufficient" (Abel 7). In fantasies, such middle-aged emergence has been well treated by Nancy Kress in *The Prince of Morning Bells* (1981) and by Le Guin in *Tehanu* (1990). Yet a coming-of-age story requires an adolescent hero, of the sort so prevalent in fiction by men. Patricia Meyer Spacks asks rhetorically where one can find female equivalents for Stephen Dedalus or Holden Caulfield and answers that one cannot, because of restrictions placed on independent young women:

> Female rebellion may be perfectly justified, but there's no good universe next door, no way out, young potential revolutionaries can't find their revolution. So they marry in defeat or go mad in a complicated form of triumph, their meaning the inevitability of failure. (158)

Realistic fiction is limited in two ways. First, it can find no "good universe next door." It is limited to the circumstances of the recognizable world, in which women have, or have had, little outlet for revolutionary or artistic impulses. Second, it is surprisingly limited in available plot lines. Marriage and madness or suicide correspond to the dramatic formulas of the comic and the tragic. These formulaic constraints exerted such control over nineteenth-century novelists that Jane Austen, who herself never married, ended every novel with multiple marriages, while George Eliot, Kate Chopin, and Edith Wharton, who all reached artistic success and a measure of economic independence, wrote of women unable to forge new social roles and driven thereby to untimely deaths.

Both formulas can, of course, result in profound and original fiction. Rachel Brownstein points out that the marriage plot, if well handled, can be used to show "how very odd it is to choose another so as to choose a self" (xvii). The heroine's selection of a proper husband may be overlaid with wit and social commentary, as in *Pride and Prejudice,* or laden with ethical implication, as in *Middlemarch.* Nonetheless, it does not show how a woman can become a self, independent of her choice of mate. It is still the story of Cinderella, waiting for the fulfillment that comes only with the right man. In a way, the realist marriage plot is worse than "Cinderella," for without the markers of fictionality—most notably magic—that are built into the fairy tale, we are encouraged to take these equally arbitrary story structures as reality.

Cinderella, along with her sisters Snow White and the Sleeping Beauty, has given fairy tales the reputation of being, for women, indoctrinations in passivity. These most familiar of fairy tale heroines all undergo intervals of confinement, metamorphosis, and reemergence as prospective wives to the more active male figures. Their rites of passage are striking echoes of those described by anthropologists, and arrive at the same ends, limiting their usefulness as models for fantasy.

Yet not all fairy tales involve heroines like Sleeping Beauty. A sizable minority of traditional tales describe a courageous, independent heroine winning her own way and reaching adulthood in the process. In Joseph Jacobs's collection *English Folk and Fairy Tales,* for instance, the following tales have young female protagonists: "Tom Tit Tot," "Nix Nought Nothing," "Cap o'Rushes," "Mollie Whuppie," "Mr. Fox," "Earl Mar's Daughter," "The Fish and the Ring," "Kate Crackernuts," "The Well of the World's End," and "The Three Heads of the Well." The heroines of these tales outwit devils, kill giants, work enchantments, work for a living, unmask false suitors, and rescue siblings. The princess in "The Three Heads of the Well" does not wait around to be rescued from an evil stepmother; instead, "The young princess having lost her father's love, grew weary of the Court, and one day, meeting with her father in the garden, she begged him, with tears in her eyes, to let her go and seek her fortune . . ." (232–33).

The unfamiliarity of tales like these is the result of a process of selection by fairy tale collectors, retellers, and editors that amounts to suppression of the independent female hero.

In the brothers Grimm's collection, which already represents a considerable editorial bias in favor of bourgeois domesticity for female characters, there remain nonetheless a handful of active heroines—which later popularizations have proceeded to weed out.

> Very few translations offer more than twenty-five tales, and thus only a handful of heroines is usually included. Most of them run the gamut from mildly abused to severely persecuted. In fact, a dozen docile heroines are the overwhelming favorites, reappearing in book after book from the mid-nineteenth century to the present. (Stone 43)

Academic folklorists have also contributed to the invisibility of the female hero. Stith Thompson's *Motif Index of Folk Literature* (1958) and Thompson and Antti Aarne's *The Types of the Folktale* (1961) illustrate a number of ways in which a supposedly objective system of classification may conceal bias. Passive verbs and nominalizations hide a number of enterprising women, so that, for instance, a tale-type with a female hero is listed by Aarne and Thompson as "The search for the lost husband" (Type 425), while the equivalent story with genders reversed is called "The man on a quest for his lost wife" (Type 400) (Lundell 154–55). The heroine's activity may even be credited to her lover, as in Type 300: "The boy rescues the princess through her magic power: She changes herself into a golden bird" (Lundell 157).

Whatever conception of female coming of age may once have been conveyed in the folktales of Europe can therefore only be imaginatively reconstructed. The evidence is hopelessly skewed, and much of it irrecoverable.

Nevertheless, the power of the folktale as narrative pattern is such that women readers and writers have devised strategies to regain it as a tool for the exploration of their own experience. Carolyn Heilbrun suggests one such strategy in the reader's refusal to limit her identification to the passive heroine, her discovery "that she is not confined to the role of the princess; that the hero, who wakens Sleeping Beauty with a kiss, is that part of herself that awakens conventional girlhood to the possibility of life and action" (150).

Heilbrun's approach is an effective one for some readers but may not be workable for all, especially young girls untrained in the art of reading subversively. Another tack is the sort of reverse discrimination practiced by editors like Ethel Johnston Phelps, whose *Tatterhood and Other Tales* (1978) assembles stories from many cultures, all featuring "heroic women distinguished by extraordinary courage and achievements, who hold the center of interest in the tales" (xv). It may be that these two approaches reinforce one another: as readers become more familiar with nonpassive heroines, they find it easier to identify with active characters of either sex.

A third strategy is the invention of original stories drawing on the motifs and structures of the traditional tale but introducing reversals of expected character roles. One of the first such stories is Jean Ingelow's largely forgotten but haunting *Mopsa the Fairy* (1869).

Ingelow was best known in her day as a poet. A friend of Browning, Ruskin, and Christina Rossetti, she seems to have shared their interest in the fairy tale as an alternative form of symbolic expression. Her only novel-length fairy tale, *Mopsa the Fairy,* reveals in its plot and symbolism some of the tensions between cultural expectations for women in the Victorian era and the aspirations of a woman writer. Many of these narrative and symbolic patterns continue to appear in fantasies by women a century later.

Ingelow's story is told primarily from the point of view of Jack, an ordinary little boy who happens one day to find a nest of fairies in a hollow tree. The four tiny fairies inside begin as infants but mature very quickly, all except for Mopsa, the one Jack kisses. She remains a child, but grows to human stature and is the only one to remain with Jack as he travels to fairyland. Jack passes through various strange realms, does a few good deeds, and meets a fairy queen. Throughout the story, Jack remains very much as he began, a polite and adventurous child. Mopsa, however, changes a great deal.

Once in the realm of the fairy queen, she matures very rapidly. She grows to Jack's height, begins to understand things that are mysteries to Jack, and initiates a sisterly rivalry with the queen. Because there cannot be two queens in one fairyland, the queen conveys a message from her mother (whose name is Fate) that Mopsa is to go rule a land where the fairies are condemned to wear the shapes of deer. Mopsa rebels, because she has heard that those fairies keep their queen imprisoned in a tower, and she and Jack flee. Finally they come, by accident, to the country of the deer, and Mopsa realizes that they want her not as a prisoner but as their deliverer. She acquiesces, and she and Jack undo the spell. The deer regain their human form, and their young prince, in honor of their rescuers, becomes Jack's exact double. Mopsa stays on to rule in her country and perhaps eventually to marry the fairy Jack. The original Jack goes home to his family.

What does all this say about a Victorian woman's coming of age? First, Ingelow uses a male protagonist to initiate her plot. *Alice in Wonderland* notwithstanding, adventures were for boys. For the first half of the book, our interest is primarily with Jack. Second, Mopsa does not become queen because of her royal birth or her innate qualities, but because Jack has kissed her: the older queen explains that "the love of a mortal works changes indeed. It is not often that we win anything so precious" (280). It is almost impossible not to read "man" for "mortal." The woman begins as something alien, a smaller imitation of a human, and only through love comes to humanity.

Third, the relationship between woman and girl is one of nurturing only until the girl grows close to womanhood and then it changes to rivalry. "I don't love the Queen," says Mopsa; "She slapped my arm as she went by, and it hurts" (294). That slap is very interesting. The red mark it leaves proves that Mopsa is indeed on her way to becoming a queen, for ordinary fairies have no red blood. The incident strongly suggests the slap often given to girls at their first menstrual cycle—one of the few ritual acts marking a girl's physical maturation in contemporary American society. In both cases, the implied message is that maturation for girls is accompanied by shame and the hostility of older women.

Fourth, Mopsa has no reliable mentor to aid her in her struggle for independence. The fairy queen is more frightening than helpful, even when giving advice: "when everyone had finished, the Queen leaned her arm on the edge of the boat and, turning her lovely face towards Mopsa, said: 'I want to whisper to you, sister.' 'Oh!' said Mopsa. 'I wish I was in

Jack's waistcoat pocket again; but I'm so big now.' And she took hold of the two sides of his velvet jacket, and hid her face between them" (304). The old apple-woman, a mortal kept by the queen as a companion, sets Mopsa on the wrong path entirely by passing on a false rumor about the deer-shaped fairies. Only when Mopsa has essentially reached her maturity does she find a wise female friend.

Fifth, whatever women need to know, they know without having to learn it. Furthermore, their knowledge is beyond logic: "Mopsa, however, was like other fairies in this respect—that she knew all about Old Mother Fate, but not about causes and reasons" (328). But when women try to tell what they know—first the queen and then Mopsa tell prophesying stories—everyone falls asleep.

Sixth, maturity for a woman involves acceptance of fate. Mopsa must reign where she is fated to reign, and any amount of wandering will only take her there in the end.

Laid out thus, the points Ingelow is making sound profoundly anti-feminist. That is not exactly the effect of the story, however. It may be read as saying that society does indeed place blocks in the path of a young woman who aspires to individuality, but that the determined heroine may overcome them. Mopsa, who begins as an ordinary young fairy, orphaned or abandoned, ends up as a queen, wiser and more humane than the fairy queen whose land she flees.

The story begins with Jack, but Mopsa and her fate are far more interesting. Jack seems to serve primarily as an avenue into the realm of the fairy tale, a conventional fairy-tale hero with a conventional name. Since more people seem to be aware of male-oriented tales than of the "Mollie Whuppie" sort of fairy tale, perhaps Ingelow thought the form required someone like Jack. Hers is not the only fantasy by a woman to begin from a male point of view. As mentioned earlier, Le Guin wrote one book about a male wizard before looking at the coming-of-age process from a female viewpoint. Patricia Wrightson's *The Ice Is Coming* (1977) and Patricia McKillip's *The Riddle-Master of Hed* (1976) also have male heroes, with female counterparts not appearing until the sequels.

What all these writers seem to be doing is reinforcing a reading like that suggested by Heilbrun for fairy tales: the male who acts as catalyst for the female's transformation is also, in a sense, herself. He represents those impulses toward independent action and self-definition which society insists the young girl suppress. Since those qualities are culturally defined as masculine, they must enter the story in male guise, but the outcome is the redefinition of the female. By the end, the heroine has grown to encompass his qualities as well as her own "masculine" initiative and "feminine" wisdom.

Virginia Woolf's fantasy *Orlando* (1928) is structured in a way that illustrates another narrative function for this device. Woolf's hero, Orlando, is male for the first half of the book, and then inexplicably changes to female. The result is that the reader is unable thereafter to view the female Orlando in the way he is accustomed to viewing female characters. We are already used to seeing Orlando travel, fight, create, fall in love, fall out of love, and so on; it is no use suddenly to start expecting him/her to become passive, mysterious, and secondary. The heroes of Le Guin's, Wrightson's, and McKillip's fantasies are male because we have come to expect the heroes of the sort of book they are in to be male. However, like Orlando, Le Guin's Ged and the others are androgynous enough that their creators can, through them, express general ideas about youth and its trials and discoveries. Then once the fantasy world is established, the writer may choose to explore the special experience of women in it.

Andre Norton, whose Witch World series waited until its third volume, *Year of the Unicorn* (1965), for a full-fledged female hero, explains why the unexamined choice of protagonist, even for a woman writer, might be male—audience expectations:

> To write a full book from the feminine point of view was a departure. I found it fascinating to write, but the reception was oddly mixed. In the years now since [*Year of the Unicorn*] was published I have had many letters from women readers who accepted Gillian with open arms, and I have had masculine readers who hotly resented her. ("On Writing Fantasy" 161)

Only when the coming of age includes sexuality does it become absolutely necessary to split the androgynous hero into male and female. Le Guin, speaking of the second book in the Earthsea trilogy, associates femininity with the sort of physical changes that were mostly left out of *A Wizard of Earthsea*:

> The subject of *The Tombs of Atuan* is, if I had to put it in one word, sex. There's a lot of symbolism in the book, most of which I did not, of course, analyze consciously while writing; the symbols can all be read as sexual. More exactly, you could call it a feminine coming of age. Birth, rebirth, destruction, freedom are the themes. (*Language* 55)

For the same reasons, Ingelow begins with Jack and moves to Mopsa when things get interesting. His kiss calls Mopsa to her fate, which then becomes the real subject of the book. The same pattern reappears in the work of more recent fantasists. In *The Tombs of Atuan*, published just about a century after Ingelow's novel, the protagonist Arha is raised as priestess of the Nameless Ones, dark, inhuman forces worshipped by her society. Her education is designed to suppress or destroy her individual personality and make her an empty vehicle for the gods she serves. When the wizard Ged arrives, he restores her humanity and individuality by giving her back the name she was born with, Tenar. That is the beginning of her rebellion and maturation. Again the male character initiates a transformation in the female, from alien to human.

Another meaning for the male catalyst emerges in Patricia Wrightson's *The Dark Bright Water* (1979). In that book, the hero from *The Ice Is Coming,* a young Aborigine named Wirrun, meets many of the creatures from his people's folklore, among them the Yunggamurra. This is a sort of fresh-water siren, a beautiful woman-shaped singer that lures men to their deaths. The Yunggamurra is not evil; her main interest is not killing men but playing in the water with her sisters. The siren song is a game she plays. After she drowns Wirrun's friend Ularra, Wirrun finds out the other rule of the game: he catches her in the smoke of a grass-fire and she is transformed from silvery water spirit to golden mortal woman: trapped, tamed, humanized.

Wrightson is making use of a traditional motif here: the swan-maiden, seal-maiden, or similar spirit creature caught by the human male, there-upon becoming his bride. But Wrightson's perspective on the story gives it a different significance. The transformed Yunggamurra, now named Murra, loves Wirrun, but she regrets her lost life: "to flow with the water and ride it; to be one strand among weeds, one voice in the singing. To rise to the sun or sink from the wind as the others do. To be no one but to be many, and to play" (216). She has given up a wild, anonymous freedom for a name and a lover.

It is an exchange Murra makes against her will, but she is willing to abide by it. However, she warns Wirrun that he must keep her away from water, where her sisters might find her: "They will call and call and I will hear and hear; and one day they will find me in water. They will catch Murra more surely than ever you caught Yunggamurra. They will take me back to the rivers and the games and I will be Yunggamurra again. You should keep me always from the water" (220).

Read as metaphor, Murra's transformation is from child to woman. Children are wild and free. They are anonymous insofar as adults fail to distinguish among them, and their identities are not fixed but fluid, responding to everything around them. A girl-child looking at her mother sees someone bounded by convention and tied to the needs of husband and children. Girl and woman might as well be different species. If the mother was once a girl, she must have been trapped and transformed. The magic spell that will do the same to her, society informs the girl, is called love.

That is one possible meaning for all these stories of witch, fairy, or animal turned into woman. In many of the traditional tales, the woman is mistreated and goes back to her old life. The man has caught her, but he does not have her soul. In a patriarchal society, that is as free as a woman can be. She accepts the bargain, lives a circumscribed life, bears her children, and becomes an adult according to her culture's dictates, but she retains an escape clause.

In *The Dark Bright Water,* Wirrun admirably refuses to play the game. He won't keep Murra locked up away from water; she is now human and must stay with him or go by her own choice. He has not sought a subservient wife but an equal companion. Much of the third volume of the trilogy concerns Murra's coming to terms with a relationship not covered by the magical game.

Jean Ingelow's fantasy does not take up such adult dilemmas, but Jack's kiss of Mopsa carries some of the same implications. Jack himself is unaware of the effect of his attentions, since men are not caught in the same way women are. By the end of the book, Mopsa has outgrown Jack (though Ingelow describes her as looking only ten years old—she has more growing to do). She has moved on to a new realm of knowledge and responsibility. Her last act in the story is to give Jack back his kiss and send him on his way home. She has accepted womanhood, but she does not tie herself to the one who triggered her transformation.

Mopsa had no older woman to guide her to maturity. The image of older woman as threatening rival rather than as mentor is familiar to us from "Hansel and Gretel" and "Snow White." This image may derive from the fact that mother and daughter must compete for favors from a dominant male. It also reflects the daughter's awareness that the mother is "in on it"—she is one of the forces pushing the girl into the constricting mold of female adulthood. In *The Tombs of Atuan,* Le Guin shows older women in the latter role. The priestess Kossil is as fearsome as any fairy-tale stepmother. She is ambitious, cruel, and hypocritical, and she resents the young priestess of the Nameless Ones, her only peer. Arha must reach adulthood literally over Kossil's dead body, when the latter is trapped in the caverns of the Nameless Ones.

Raederle, the heroine of Patricia McKillip's *Heir of Sea and Fire* (1977), has both positive and negative role models among older women. The old pig-woman, who is really the wizard Nun in disguise (McKillip's wizards can be female), gives her friendship and instruction in the magical arts. On the other hand, the shapechanger Eriel attacks Raederle's lover

Morgon and taunts Raederle with the idea that Raederle will eventually become as ruthless as she. Both are magicians, and both are kin to Raederle. Nun represents the mother Raederle would like to be like; Eriel is the mother she dreads becoming. Raederle's own mother is dead, and so the story of her coming of age is also the story of her search for an acceptable maternal model, just as many male fantasy heroes are looking for fathers. In addition, Raederle's shapechanger heritage echoes the common fantasy treatment of women as alien creatures until they are tamed by love.

Raederle's problem is learning to accept and control the powers she was born with, whereas her male counterpart Morgon must learn his powers step by step. This distinction between acquired and inborn ability or knowledge marks many fantasies by and about women. As mentioned earlier, Mopsa begins to know things spontaneously when she reaches a certain level of maturity, and this knowledge is of a sort that cannot be explained to Jack. The fantasies are here echoing a common perception of women as intuitive, men as logical.

Michelle Zimbalist Rosaldo, examining this idea in a cultural context, suggests two explanations. Women's knowledge is perceived as illogical and unsystematic, she suggests, because cultures do not develop complex categories for women's activities as they do for men's: "It is because men enter the world of articulated social relations that they appear to us as intellectual, rational, or instrumental; and the fact that women are excluded from that world makes them seem to think and behave in another mode" (30). Women appear to acquire their knowledge spontaneously because they have been learning it by imitation since infancy, whereas "a man's experience lacks this continuity; he may be wrenched from the domestic sphere in which he spent his earliest years, by means of rituals or initiations that teach him to distrust or despise the world of his mother, to seek his manhood outside the home" (28).

Although women in fantasies are represented as possessing this intuitive understanding, to rely entirely on such knowledge would leave them reproducing the lives of their mothers. Some additional knowledge is required if the cycle is to be broken, and, since men have always had to break away from the maternal world, the female heroes of fantasy borrow knowledge from them. Already knowing of continuity, duty, and the submersion of the self, they must learn of individuality and rebellion; hence Ged gives to the priestess Arha (translated as "the eaten one") her birth name of Tenar. Hence Wirrun gives to the Yunggamurra, who has no identity distinct from her race, the individual name of Murra.

Armed with a double knowledge, these heroes can grow into mature, independent women, sometimes into magic-workers and queens. They are free to choose their roles, although they may have been fated to those roles all along, as Mopsa was fated to rule over her realm. If she had merely acquiesced in her fate and gone meekly to the land of the fairies who had been turned into deer, they would never have been freed from their enchantment. The spell required that "They were to remain in the disguise of deer till a queen of alien birth should come to them against her will" (328). Mopsa's rebellion made her the queen they needed.

In a few very recent works, women characters come of age in ways different from that mapped out in *Mopsa the Fairy*. No male characters are required to initiate the plots of Diana Wynne Jones's *The Spell-coats* (1979), Virginia Hamilton's *Justice and Her Brothers* (1978), Michaela Roessner's *Walkabout Woman* (1988), and Suzette Haden Elgin's Ozark trilogy (1981). Nor are their women characters portrayed as something other than human to begin with, though they may grow into something greater than human.

Responsible of Brightwater, the heroine of Elgin's trilogy, is on center stage from the beginning. She needs no man to teach her independence. Fourteen years old at the beginning of the series, she possesses an adolescent self-assurance not always short of arrogance. She has her magical powers well in hand and is fully supplied with female mentors in the persons of the Grannys [*sic*] who run households on the planet Ozark. Ozark society is organized in a fashion derived from its earthly namesake: men and women inhabit largely separate spheres, with the men handling politics, feuds, food-raising, and major magical spells, and the women concerned with household maintenance, child rearing, the preservation of knowledge, and small bits of "Granny Magic." What the men do not know is that there is always one woman, always named Responsible, who is the "meta-magician" of Ozark. She can do anything the male Magicians of Rank can do and more. She is the channel through which magical powers reach the magicians. The Grannys know all this, but they have been content for generations to let the men think they run things: the attitude is that male egos are too frail to handle too much truth.

Here is how one Granny explains the difference between the sexes:

"If," she said, "a man does something properly, that's an accident. That's the first thing. As for the sorry messes they make in the ordinary way of things, that's to be expected, and not to be held against them—they can't help it. That's the second thing. And the third thing—and this is to be *well-remembered*—is that no man must ever know the first two things. . . ."

"And a woman?" one of the little girls had asked timidly. "How about a woman?"

The Granny had gripped her cane till her knuckles gleamed like pearls. "There is *nothing*," she said in a terrible voice like ice grinding together, "more despicable than a woman who cannot *Cope!*" (*Jubilee* 259)

Within this separate but unequal system, a woman can reach a state of considerable maturity and even power, so Elgin can write about Responsible of Brightwater without relying on a male hero to set the story into motion or to act as a catalyst in her maturation. The quest that takes up the first book and sets the seal on her adulthood is her own idea. No man names her, either; that is a task for Grannys and one of the most important aspects of their magic. However, coming of age also includes coming to terms with sexuality, either outright or in symbolic guise.

There is one man on Ozark who is a suitable match for Responsible: Lewis Motley Wommack the 33rd is handsome, charismatic, and as unorthodox as she. They meet and are attracted to one another, but her independence irks him. There is no room in the worldview he has been taught for such a strong woman. They seduce one another, with different motivations, and along with sexual conjunction comes close psychic communion. For her, the experience is pleasurable:

> Sure enough, it had been a kind of peace, a kind of wondrous *rest,* being with someone whose mind she could share as easily as she shared ordinary speech with everybody else. Like moving around in a place of columns and soft wind and— She brought herself up short. If there'd been words for what it was like, it wouldn't have been what it was. . . . (*Jubilee,* 367)

Wommack, however, does not like this invasion of his mind. Too proud simply to ask Responsible to get out, he calls in the Magicians of Rank to end it. They put Responsible into a magical sleep (Prince Charming in reverse), with disastrous results. Responsible is able to handle anything having to do with magic, but there is no satisfactory solution to love in a culture that treats men and women as separate species. Lewis Motley Wommack places Responsible and the planet into great peril that cannot be averted by any effort of the male Magicians. Instead, the problem is solved by two other young women, Responsible's sister Troublesome and the saintly Silverweb of McDaniels.

What Elgin has done is reverse the traditional distinction between men, who undergo ordeals and become fully adult, and women, who do not. Responsible, Troublesome, Silverweb, and the other young women we meet go through ordeals, both ritual and real, and are ready to meet the obligations of adulthood. The men, though, are too well protected by the Grannys and other women. They live their lives in a pleasant illusion of mastery. Unlike most earlier writers of fantasy, Elgin does not treat the society of women as something to be escaped or outgrown. Although Responsible has negative role models in her mother and in the one renegade Granny, Granny Leeward, she is generally well supported and instructed by the women she meets. Granny Leeward, and not Lewis Motley Wommack or the Magicians of Rank, is her chief adversary because she is a woman: she knows the true state of things and still chooses mischief, whereas the men are simply blundering as usual. Elgin treats men, not women, as a semi-alien race. Like the mules (an intelligent native species outwardly resembling our mules and condescending to be used as beasts of burden), men are capricious and balky. Both can be managed, but not really communicated with. The mules are generally considered to have more sense.

No earlier fantasy that I know of is told so squarely from a woman's perspective. The world of Ozark incorporates the rituals, institutions, and insights that early anthropologists thought women lacked. Having shown that women do indeed come of age, Elgin next points out the necessity of adapting society to accommodate the resulting adult woman. Responsible of Brightwater deserves the company of a man who will not confuse communion with invasion or courtesy with capitulation.

It is possible to go beyond Elgin's formulation of the female coming-of-age story, but only by positing a vastly different world from even our comparatively feminized one. This is a step that fantasy has been reluctant to take, but science fiction provides many examples of all-women, androgynous, or nonsexist societies and the development of young heroines within them. Science fiction readily proposes changes in economic systems, family structures, political relationships, even language (such as David Gerrold's unnerving use of single pronoun *she* for characters of either sex in his 1977 novel *Moonstar Odyssey*). Fantasy's reliance on traditional motifs makes it less adaptable to such wholesale transformations of society; it usually focuses on the development of the exceptional individual rather than the reformation of culture. It is probably not accidental that Elgin's Ozark trilogy, unlike the other stories discussed in this chapter, is really science fantasy, combining the magic of fantasy with the future setting and technological underpinnings of science fiction. Science fantasy can do many things that traditional fantasy cannot; some of those will be taken up in the next chapter.

But even without remaking every cultural institution, fantasy can call certain assumptions into question. It can begin with inherited story structures and direct them toward unexpected ends, turning Cinderellas into Princesses Charming and waking sleeping strengths in Sleeping Beauties. Its very avoidance of the details of contemporary society gives it flexibility, for its heroines need not carry such cultural burdens as women's economic dependency, religious rationales for the suppression of women, and the commercial exploitation of women as sex objects. Freed of these, heroines have a chance of coping with personal relationships and with their own limitations.

Individually composed narratives like these are not an exact analog of culturally sanctioned rites of passage, but they serve to remind us of the ritual process and its value to the individual. Though lacking the authority of ritual, narratives are in some ways better suited to the needs of an evolving society. Because a reader undergoes only a vicarious induction into a new identity, that identity remains provisional and subject to further testing and growth. As such narratives proliferate, they serve to complement and comment upon one another.

When we follow Mopsa's path from toy-like creature to queen, we see how the extraordinary individual may defy societal expectations to achieve self-determination. When we follow Responsible as she comes to terms with her own power and authority, we see how the hidden operations of a culture may oppose its own official institutions to offer support to the emerging self. Each of the narratives considered here describes a different route to maturity and defines it in different terms: physical, emotional, metaphysical, political. Some of the heroes do, like their fairy tale predecessors, mark their passage by marriage, but in no case does marriage constitute or justify their achievements.

None of them fail in their quests for expanded knowledge and scope of action. Because the conventions of fantasy require that a task undertaken be completed within the narrative, the outcome may, especially in formula fantasy, seem forced or inadequate to the problems posed. It will not, however, be the madness, suicide, or despair that seem the lot of the realistic heroine. In the works considered here, there is no forcing: maturity is hard-won but worth the winning, and the female heroes represent an unprecedented range of models for development. Their success in emerging as women of power and self-knowledge makes them more universal, as well: the male reader (like myself) can adopt Carolyn Heilbrun's strategy and, by identifying with Tenar or Raederle or Responsible, learn more truly what it means to come of age.

SEVEN

Science Fantasy

FOR SEVERAL YEARS, fantasy has shared shelf space in bookstores with science fiction: retailers assume that the two forms attract the same or overlapping audiences. More recently, many of the books on those shelves fit both categories at once. Booksellers and publishers, who like such books because they appeal to a broader segment of the fantasy/science fiction market than do either pure fantasy or hard-core science fiction, generally label the hybrid science fantasy. Writers, who tend to resist labels, nonetheless like the possibilities science fantasy offers. Just as both science fiction and fantasy may range from blatant imitations of imitations to wild innovation, science fantasy, though it has already developed some of the deadlier formulas, has also generated some of the most interesting stylistic, narratological, and epistemological experimentation in contemporary fiction.

Fantasy and science fiction run in parallel for much of their development. Many of the same writers contributed to both: Edgar Allan Poe, Nathaniel Hawthorne, and Mark Twain wrote sketches that contributed to the early development of science fiction, but all three worked with nonscientific fantasy as well. H. G. Wells is the author of "The Man Who Could Work Miracles" as well as *The Time Machine*. Among contemporary writers, Ursula K. Le Guin, Andre Norton, Gene Wolfe, Patricia McKillip, Samuel Delany, and John Crowley are representative of the successful switch-hitters.

With so much shared history, it is not surprising that science fiction and fantasy overlap so frequently. Science fantasy is the area of that overlap. As a hybrid form, it can with equal justice be defined either as a form of fantasy that borrows from science fiction or as a subgenre of science fiction drawing inspiration from fantasy. Moreover, as a hybrid, it can be reinvented again and again as both science fiction and fantasy develop. It is always more clearly related to the current forms of its parent genres than to prior science fantasies. Each time the cross is made, the result is a fictional form able to make use of the conventions of science fiction and those of genre fantasy to comment on one another and on the worldview implied by each form of storytelling.

Because there are already many histories and a few good theoretical works dealing with science fiction, I need give only a brief summary here of its nature and development. Science fiction shares with fantasy a long prehistory of traditional story forms: Odysseus's voyage and Icarus's flight are precursors of both modern genres, as are tales of golems and other artificial beings, changeling legends, utopias, dream visions, and allegories. Science fiction began to separate from fantasy when science began to deliver on the promises made by alchemists and magicians. Mary Shelley's *Frankenstein* (1818), often cited as the first science fiction novel, drew upon Gothic atmosphere and Greek myth, but Shelley substituted electricity for divine fire, the laboratory for the haunted monastery, and the scientist for demon or demigod. Thus a new genre was constructed from pieces of the old.

Science fiction, like fantasy, is easier to recognize than to describe formally. Viewed as a fuzzy set, it clusters around representative texts like H. G. Wells's *The Time Machine* (1895), E. E. "Doc" Smith's Skylark series (1928–66), Robert E. Heinlein's *Citizen of the Galaxy* (1957), Arthur C. Clarke's *Rendezvous with Rama* (1973), Anne McCaffrey's *Dragonflight* (1968), and Ursula K. Le Guin's *The Left Hand of Darkness* (1969). More precisely, each of those titles represents a set within the larger set of science fiction. Texts resembling those I have named could be called, respectively, classic or sociological SF, space opera, Golden Age SF, hard-core or technological SF, science fantasy, and New Wave or literary SF.

Critics trying to make unity out of this multiplexity have proposed a number of useful terms, such as "extrapolation" and Darko Suvin's "cognitive estrangement" (4), but no such term covers all the examples. Wells is clearly extrapolative: he looks for trends in the society of his day and extends the pattern into a hypothetical future. McCaffrey's Dragon books are just as clearly not extrapolative: nothing in our world would lead us to anticipate the planet of Pern, with its devouring Thread and soaring dragons. Likewise, Le Guin effectively "estranges" us from conventional gender roles: we turn from her world of Winter to the world surrounding us and both look strange, unlikely, awkward, and fascinating. Yet Heinlein does nothing of the sort: instead, he makes the universe into an extension of our own neighborhood.

If there is any common thread among science fiction texts, it is their use of a particular language or discourse. The "science" part of the term often seems inappropriate, since neither the methods nor the accumulated knowledge of scientists is accurately portrayed in many texts that are nevertheless solidly within the genre. However, if scientific knowledge may be flouted, scientific terminology reigns supreme, even in the most non-cognitive space opera. "Magic" is not part of the language of SF; "telepathy" is. "Faster-than-light travel" may be an impossibility, according to our understanding of physics, but the term itself has a scientific ring that justifies its use in science fiction.

The vocabulary of science is only part of the discourse of science fiction. Other parts of the discourse include a set of recurring images that Gary K. Wolfe calls "icons" (*Known* 16): the robot, the monster, the barrier, the city; all conveying in concrete form science's way of relating the human self to the unknown universe. Likewise, the conventional settings of SF, from the rocket ship to the galactic empire, refer directly to present or past states of scientific knowledge about the universe. And its recurring situations—First Contact, Time-Travel Paradox, Conceptual Breakthrough—invoke scientific paradigms and shifts in paradigms. One function of this discourse is to make both science and previous science fiction serve as background information for the SF reader. Or rather, since it is more important than mere background and often more interesting than the supposed foreground of character and plot, science serves as a megatext for each SF text. Science surrounds, supports, and judges SF in much the same way the Bible grounds Christian devotional poetry. It does not matter much if specific scientific references within the story are bogus, so long as the discourse is able to call upon the megatext.

Evoking science in this fashion can serve several functions. For readers who consider themselves among its initiates, including most early fans, the scientific references can suggest a Galilean devotion to truth in the face of ignorance and orthodoxy, as in Isaac Asimov's "Nightfall" (1941). For the public at large, which recognizes airplanes, automobiles, vaccines, and computers as products of science, the science megatext promises un-limited movement, adventure, and control of one's environment. For writers, it greatly multiplies one's options in generating plots, characters, and settings. It encourages speculation about social systems and individual identities through extrapolation or analogy or a combination of the two. The discourse of science fiction may even call science itself into question, either its applications, as in *Frankenstein,* or its claims to objective validity, as in Stanislav Lem's *Solaris* (1961).

Yet SF is also limited by its reliance on the megatext of science. It becomes less and less possible to write about certain things and still call upon that megatext. Interstellar travel, contact with aliens, colonization of other planets; science has begun to cast doubt on whether any number of technological breakthroughs would make these fictional standbys facts. They may join Martian canals and lost civilizations as no-longer-effective springboards for the imagination, at least within the discourse of SF.

Not only has SF lost some of its power, it has also lost its innocence in a world in which the products of science include horrifying war machines and seas of waste. SF has always had both optimistic and pessimistic strains, both *A Modern Utopia* and *The Time Machine,* but the difference has been largely a matter of one's view of human nature, not of the capability and fitness of science itself. Now, however, some writers seem to have lost faith in the scientific imagination, looking outside the scientific megatext for other ways of seeing and judging. Yet there are very few alternative megatexts sufficiently powerful, comprehensive, and familiar to act as a commentary on science. Even religion lacks the authority it once had for many readers, because it cannot match the material payoffs provided by science.

The discourse of fantasy can challenge SF, partly because it pays its own tribute to science. Impossibility itself, one of the elements of fantasy, is defined largely through reference to the current scientific worldview, especially where that coincides with common sense. Because it is the *current* view of reality that is violated in a fantasy, inventions that were once fantastic may be no longer, or vice versa. The transmutation of metals might serve as an example of both sorts of change: once part of science, then impossible, and now achieved. Nonetheless, we can tell whether the transmutation is to be viewed as possible or not by the discourse that surrounds it. If an alchemist's description of the philosopher's stone were inserted verbatim into a modern fantasy, it would cease to testify to the existence of such a miraculous substance and become part of the rhetoric of the unreal. The same description within a science fiction text might be used to represent exploded myth or to highlight the mysterious properties of transuranic metals.

If fantasy were only the denial of science, however, there would be no contest between them. But in affirming impossibility, fantasy opens the door to mythology, which is the name we give to cast-off megatexts. Gods, fairies, ancestor spirits, charms, spells: a whole host of motifs no longer convey belief and yet retain their narrative momentum and—and here is one of the great differences between science fiction and fantasy—their congruence with the ways we wish we saw the world. They are emotionally and psychologically, if not scientifically, valid, and therefore most potent where science fiction is traditionally weakest.

Most science fiction texts are essentially extroverted: concerned with behavior, physical environment, and the mechanisms of society. The discourse itself calls attention to the effect of scientific ideas on present and future actions. The characteristic narrative mode of SF, accordingly, is naturalistic, emphasizing external action, plausibility, and orderly chains of cause and effect. When SF does take up psychological themes, it is usually in relation to their physiological causes or sociological implications. Very little SF is predicated on the science of psychology itself, which may suggest that psychology is more discourse than science.

If science fiction's gaze is outward and ahead, fantasy's is inward and into the past. The discourse of fantasy encourages borrowings from folk literatures, most frequently from European fairy tales, Celtic legendry, Norse epic, and various bodies of myth. Because these traditional narratives have shed whatever external referentiality they once had for their listeners, their internal dynamics become all the more important as expressions of psychological processes. One way of connecting fantasy with experience is to see the fantasy world as a map of the mind, and the conflict taking place there as something like a medieval psychomachia, a contest between personified virtues and vices, or in more modern terms between integrative and destructive forces within the personality.

When we contrast fantasy and science fiction, the rhetoric of each becomes more evident. For example, the emphasis on material causes in SF finds its counterpart within fantasy in the assumption of immaterial connections. In a fantasy, invisible chains link a ring and a dark fortress, or a star-shaped birthmark and the stars inlaid on a harp. These intangible connections reflect emotional or metaphoric associations, rather than demonstrable causative ties. Fantasy refers to them as magic; in a visionary poem they might be called correspondences. The pure strain of fantasy has less in common with naturalistic narrative, of which science fiction is a subspecies, than with the work of Blake or Rimbaud or Roethke. The naturalistic impulse is to undo these metaphoric connections, to see not resemblances but accidental associations, not correspondences but parallel results of forces like gravity or greed, history or hunger.

Science fiction owes much of its power to the reader's sense of being able to arrive at the fictional world by following current trends to their natural conclusion. Indeed, science fiction is so much a mirror of the writer's own time and place that SF stories from the turn of the century or the 1950s could be used by historians as documents of vanished worldviews, of futures past. Fantasy, on the other hand, posits a barrier between the fictional universe and the reader's own. Because the fantasy world and the axioms that underlie it are radically unlike our own, the reader is forced to seek connections in other than rational, external directions, relating the portrayed reality instead to myth, dream, and other manifestations of psychological or metaphysical principles. Fantasies too are products of particular places and times, but what they document is the way a culture conceives the formation of a self from assembled experiences, instincts, and internalized cultural constructs.

These differences in discourse might make it seem difficult to blend SF and fantasy, and indeed a common critical judgment says that they should not be mixed. Ursula K. Le Guin is reflecting this judgment when she criticizes her own early novel, *Rocannon's World* (1966):

> There is a lot of promiscuous mixing going on in *Rocannon's World*. We have NAFAL and FTL spaceships, we also have Brisingamen's necklace, windsteeds, and some imbecilic angels. We have an extremely useful garment called an impermasuit, resistant to "foreign elements, extreme temperatures, radioactivity, shocks, and blows of moderate velocity and weight such as swordstrokes or bullets," and inside which the wearer would die of suffocation within five minutes. The impermasuit is a good example of where fantasy and science fiction *don't* shade gracefully into one another. A symbol from collective fantasy— the Cloak of Protection (invisibility, etc.)—is decked out with some pseudoscientific verbiage and a bit of vivid description, and passed off as a marvel of Future Technology. This can be done triumphantly if the symbol goes deep enough (Wells's Time Machine), but if it's merely decorative or convenient, it's cheating. It degrades both symbol and science. . . . (134–35)

It is true that many writers of science fantasy seem perfectly willing to cheat. A typical novel by Jack Chalker or Piers Anthony is rife with shortcuts and easy answers. The science is bogus; the fantasy insincere. Darko Suvin, whose discussions of science fiction emphasize its cognitive dimension, sees any intrusion of fantasy as a weakening of that function: he calls science fantasy a "misshapen subgenre" (68), and his judgment is borne out by its worst examples. But superimposing the discourse of science fiction on that of fantasy need not merely compound the potential flaws in both genres. In the hands of a Roger Zelazny or a Gene Wolfe, the mixed mode may combine the intellectual rigor of fine science fiction with the profundity of the best symbolic fantasy, and it may take on qualities unique to itself as well.

The success of science fantasy depends on the writer's ability to handle two kinds of structure independently yet simultaneously. When this happens, and the two forms of discourse are given approximately equal weight, a third level of meaning develops as the voices of science fiction and fantasy are perceived by the reader to interact with and comment upon one another.

The task is made a little easier by the fact that many of the characteristic motifs of fantasy reappear in science fiction in other guises. Immortality may be represented as being achieved through pharmacology; prophecy may be termed precognition; spells of illusion may be explained as the amplification and projection of brain waves. Each of these motifs has both an inner significance and an outer, which can be exploited respectively by fantasy and science fiction. Science fiction is able to make us perceive a fantastic idea as something reasonable and even likely, given enough time to work out the mechanics, while fantasy can take something that already exists and make it seem miraculous. In both cases, the operation is a matter of rhetoric: the way an idea is introduced, the vocabulary used to describe it, the manner in which it is made into an element of the story.

In many science fantasies, each of the two forms of discourse attempts to account for the other. Sometimes one side is more convincing. If the favored pattern is science fictional, the result is not so much science fantasy as rationalized fantasy: the apparent magic is effectively explained away by the end of the story, the curtain drawn back to reveal the technological apparatus responsible for each miracle, as in Robert Heinlein's *Glory Road* (1964). Or the rhetoric of fantasy may prove the stronger, in which case the science-fictional discourse may turn into a one-sided frame that introduces the actual story but does not close it off at the end. This is the case with C. S. Lewis's *Out of the Silent Planet* (1938), which begins with a spaceship and ends with angels. Rarely are the two rhetorical modes in absolute balance, though the tensions that give science fantasy its hybrid vigor are most evident in the works that allow no easy dismissal of either viewpoint.

Among works that mingle the rhetoric of science fiction with that of fantasy, nearly all can be classed as either humorous or mythological. A number, such as L. Sprague de Camp and Fletcher Pratt's Incomplete Enchanter novellas, are both. Why should science fantasies tend toward these seemingly unrelated perspectives? One answer is that both humor and myth are products of the linguistic and perceptual disjunction that characterizes science fantasy.

The humorous possibilities of the form were not recognized immediately. Edgar Rice Burroughs was one of the first to fuse fantasy and science fiction, beginning with his *A Princess of Mars,* serialized as "Under the Moons of Mars" in 1912. The formula developed in this book and reproduced in endless sequels involved transporting human heroes to exotic settings ostensibly based on astronomical observation but more closely akin to the lost-world fantasies of H. Rider Haggard. By using the terminology of science fiction for the apparatus of fantasy, Burroughs freed himself from most of the obligations of both forms. Where fantasy would restrict him to ethical consistency or narrative closure, he turns to the open-endedness of science fiction. Where science fiction would restrict him to the laws of biology or physics, he claims immunity under the dispensation of fantasy.

The humor implicit in science fantasy is already there in Burroughs's work, though he himself was generally unaware of it. His disregard of fact led him to commit scenes of hilarity no less enjoyable for being unintentional. In an introduction to one of her own works of science fantasy, Marion Zimmer Bradley describes her reaction to his blithely proposing a love interest between an earth man and an egg-laying Martian (in a scene actually from the first volume, *A Princess of Mars*):

> I was trained as a biologist—which probably protected me when people thought the old pulp magazine covers were immoral, with a bug-eyed monster carrying off a lightly draped maiden; I knew, if nobody else did, that the Bug-eyed Monster could not possibly have Evil Designs upon the Maiden—except, perhaps, to treat her as dinner, not as a Sex Object. I had giggled uncontrollably, reading the second of the John Carter of Mars books, in which John Carter and his beloved Martian Princess (what the heck was her name? Thuvia?) were standing hand in hand, sentimentally regarding their unhatched egg. (viii)

It remained only for writers following Burroughs to exploit systematically the incongruities he introduced unknowingly. The writers who did so emerged from the pulp magazine tradition for which Burroughs is in large part responsible. When Burroughs began writing, no specialized science fiction or fantasy magazine existed: the first Mars story appeared in a general adventure-story pulp called *All-Story*. By 1926, however, Hugo Gernsback had started his pioneering *Amazing Stories,* in which the later Mars books appeared. The genealogy of the pulps is complex, but, to trace one line of descent, *Amazing Stories* in 1930 discovered a young writer named John Campbell. Campbell went on to edit *Astounding Science-Fiction,* which under his direction became the most prestigious outlet for serious extrapolative fiction. Perhaps for relief from such sobriety, Campbell founded a companion fantasy magazine, *Unknown,* in 1939, and it is that magazine's brief run that created a vogue for humorous science fantasy.

One of the most engaging of the *Unknown* writers was Fredric Brown.

In his introduction to *Angels and Spaceships* (1954), a collection of
stories originally published in the two Campbell magazines, he discusses
the two directions taken by his fiction, which correspond to the markets
for which he wrote:

> Fantasy deals with things that are not and that cannot be.
>   Science fiction deals with things that can be, that someday may be.
> Science fiction confines itself to possibilities within the realm of logic. (1)

Science fiction, he goes on to say, requires explanation or at least the
impression of it, while in fantasy the vampire, demon, or angel is accepted
without question.

When Brown describes the stories in his collection, he says that "the
stories in this book divide about equally between fantasy and science
fiction. By which I mean that some are clearly one, some clearly the other,
and a few fall in between" (3).

Many of Brown's stories are funny, but these in-betweens, or science
fantasies, are a cut above his usual mild satire. Brown had a generous
stock of comic devices—puns, hallucinations, inebriated ad writers—that
he threw freely into all kinds of stories. The science fantasies, though,
exploit a distinctive line of humor, one that grows out of their hybrid
nature. In these stories science fiction meets fantasy: a linotype machine
achieves enlightenment, an "automatonic autosuggestive subvibratory su-
peraccelerator" calls up a shy genie, and heaven proves to be a super
printshop. In each case, the humor depends on a sudden reversal of our
expectations. If the story has been developing rationally, extrapolating
from some reasonable assumption, the twist will be magical. If we think
we are in a fairy tale, a bit of commonsense ingenuity will short-circuit the
pattern.

For example, Brown describes a surprising transformation witnessed
by the hero of one story, "The Angelic Angleworm," as he prepares for a
fishing trip:

> His fingertips came together, but there wasn't a worm between them,
> because something had happened to the worm. When he'd reached out for
> it, it had been a quite ordinary-looking angleworm. It most definitely had
> not had a pair of wings. Nor a—
>   It was quite impossible, of course, and he was dreaming or seeing
> things, but there it was.
>   Fluttering upward in a graceful slow spiral that seemed utterly
> effortless. Flying past Charlie's face with wings that were shimmery-white,
> and not at all like butterfly wings or bird wings but like—
>   Up and up it circled, now above Charlie's head, now level with the roof

of the house, then a mere white—somehow a *shining* white—speck against the gray sky. And after it was out of sight, Charlie's eyes still looked upward. (115–16)

This luminous, silly image is typical of the comic side of science fantasy. Its effect depends on two sets of associations. First, the worm is linked with scientific and commonsense reality: worms provide our first lesson in predation as we watch robins yanking them from wet lawns; their corpses are our first dissections in biology class; and they remind us that human beings too are part of the food chain. Second, this worm's wings and the halo that Charlie can't quite bring himself to name represent escape from the natural order. The sudden swoop from nature to the supernatural, from burrowing in the earth to flying toward heaven, from death and corruption to shining immortality, is funny. A mythic treatment of the same image can be found in George MacDonald's *Lilith* (1895).

The scene precisely fits Arthur Koestler's analysis of the intellectual structure of humor:

> It is the sudden clash between . . . two mutually exclusive codes of rules— or associative contexts—that produces the comic effect. It compels the listener to perceive the situation in two self-consistent but incompatible frames of reference at the same time; his mind has to operate simultaneously on two different wavelengths. ("Humor and Wit," 1974)

Koestler calls this process "bisociation." Humor results from the sudden dissolving of a seemingly stable pattern and its resolution into another pattern based on entirely different assumptions. In this case, the assumptions of science dissolve into those of fantasy, but not without strain; the strain is relieved by humor.

In a pun, words with similar sounds provide the bisociative hinge, swinging us suddenly into another plane of reference. It is probably not accidental that most comic science fantasies are rife with puns. Piers Anthony's Xanth novels, for example, are built on little else. In Brown's story "The Angelic Angleworm," it is an image, a sort of visual pun reinforced by the verbal play on *angle/angel,* that forces us to bisociate. In more fully developed science fantasies, characters and plot elements can add to the confusion by functioning simultaneously within the conventions of science fiction and those of fantasy.

The humorous effect of blending the two forms of discourse was exploited in this more complex fashion by de Camp and Pratt in their series of tales about Harold Shea, the Incomplete Enchanter. The first of these novellas, "The Roaring Trumpet," appeared in *Unknown* in 1941 and helped set that magazine's characteristic tone of tongue-in-cheek wonderment. In de Camp and Pratt's story, Harold Shea, a psychologist from Ohio, sets out to test a theory that our perceptions are dependent on our assumptions about reality: change the assumptions and you change the perceptions; change the perceptions and you shift universes. Shea's mathematical formulas propel him into the world of Norse mythology just before Ragnarok, the final battle between gods and giants.

In this milieu, Shea acts as the comic stooge because he insists on applying technology where only magic works. He suffers successive humiliations when he attempts to use a flashlight, matches, a gun, and that textbook of basic science, the Boy Scout Manual. When he is not making a fool of himself clicking a nonfunctional firearm at a dragon, he is with equal thick-headedness failing to reckon with or even recognize the supernatural forces in operation around him.

When Shea at last redeems himself, it is by combining psychology and magic. Finally realizing that the magic in this universe has its own logical consistency, he is able to cast a spell to free himself and his companion Heimdall, performing a little plastic surgery by sympathetic magic on their troll jailer. Having made a small contribution to the cause of the gods, he is accidentally ejected from the Norse universe just before the serious apocalyptic action gets going. De Camp and Pratt seem to have decided their narrative vehicle was too flimsy to include real mythological action, and so they used some variant of that eleventh-hour escape in all the subsequent Harold Shea novellas.

What makes the story so funny? Juxtapositions of all kinds, from Shea's anachronistic diction to his confrontation with gods he doesn't really believe in. Shea is a humorous character not because he is a bumbling fool but because the conventional wisdom of science betrays him. After he catches on to the workings of magic and learns to adapt his worldview to circumstances, he ceases to be the butt of the joke, and in the sequels other greenhorns must be thrown in to take his place as the representative of misapplied learning: Reed Chalmers in "The Mathematics of Magic" (1940), Vaclav Polacek in "The Castle of Iron" (1941), Walter Bayard in "The Wall of Serpents" (1953), and Pete Brodsky in "The Green Magician" (1954).

There is also plot-based humor in the Harold Shea stories. The two basic patterns for humorous incidents are the unexpected escalation, or sorcerer's apprentice motif, and the anticlimax, or dud firecracker. Every time Shea or one of his later substitutes attempts to perform a magical transformation, we can expect the results to be either too much or too little, ridiculously so in either case. Sometimes the result is at once too much *and* too little, as when Reed Chalmers attempts to produce a dragon and gets, first, a hundred placidly herbivorous specimens and, later, one properly fierce fire-breather the size of a chicken.

The humor in both cases is based on violation of expectations explicitly raised by the rhetorical structure. At first de Camp and Pratt were burlesquing a formula, so that the audience could be expected to know with a minimum of clues that a given sequence was supposed to end with an act of violence or a sudden inspiration on the part of the hero. By simply following the formula to the moment of crisis and having nothing at all happen, they could provoke an audience reaction, as Kant described the humorous response, "arising from the sudden transformation of a strained expectation into nothing" (*The Critique of Judgment,* trans. J. H. Bernard, quoted by Max Eastman, 153). When that humorous device itself became expected, as the burlesque of formula became established as another formula, it could be just as disconcerting, and therefore as funny, to have a smug expectation of nothing transformed into something.

When we juxtapose magic and science, they may seem at first to be so unlike one another as to be incompatible, but the best part of de Camp and Pratt's joke is that they are really quite similar, or can be made to seem so through carefully parallel rhetorical frameworks. Shea's particular brand of science, psychology, works quite well in the various magic worlds he visits, because its techniques—the use of arcane words, hypnotic gestures, and elaborate metaphors to manipulate unseen forces—are also those of the enchanter. Likewise, abstract mathematical formulas, like "If either P or Q is true or (Q or R) is true then either Q is true or (P or R) is false—"(*The Compleat Enchanter* 12), are, to the uninitiated, nothing more than variations on "abracadabra" or "hocus-pocus," and so Reed Chalmers can turn himself into a powerful sorcerer using symbolic logic.

The formula developed by de Camp and Pratt has been taken up by many other writers. Among the stories that owe a debt to the Incomplete Enchanter series are Keith Laumer's Lafayette O'Leary novels beginning with *The Time Bender* (1981), Gordon Dickson's *The Dragon and the George* (1976), Christopher Stasheff's *The Warlock in Spite of Himself* (1969) and its sequels, and James Schmitz's *The Witches of Karres* (1966).

Suzette Haden Elgin's Ozark trilogy draws on the formula but at the same time reinvigorates it through the application of a new science, linguistics. Ozark is a world that most of its inhabitants take for purely magical. Only Elgin's heroine knows that the flying mules and other spells are—I was going to say explainable by science, but that is not it exactly. Rather, magic and science seem to be parallel systems of meaning, translatable into one another and subject to the same metalinguistic rules. Elgin reinforces this view by modeling her magic spells after operations of transformational grammar, which are more than a little reminiscent of Harold Shea's symbolic logic.

> "Let there be," I said over the whole, "a name, sub-N; and let there be a filling of the null term, sub-T; and let there be no alteration of the underlying structure, sub-S!" (*Twelve Fair Kingdoms* 164)

But Elgin does not merely use her linguistic science as hocus-pocus. Reflecting her own academic training, her transformations are scrupulously worked out to indicate the linguistic underpinnings of the magical operations of Insertion, Deletion, Movement, and Substitution. By proposing the simple but far-reaching assumption that grammatical structure governs, rather than simply imitating, the thing described, Elgin reunites grammar with its cognates *gramarye* and *glamour*. On Planet Ozark, anyone with the knowledge and gift can perform arcane operations on the deep structure of reality, so long as she remembers the fundamental constraint: "it is not *allowed, ever,* to change the Meaning of things" (165–66). A basic principle of transformational grammar thus echoes the injunctions of serious fantasy.

In using linguistics as the scientific side of science fantasy, Elgin underlines the rhetorical basis of her story. The reader is alerted to the role of grammatical juxtapositions in determining points of view when such juxtapositions directly affect the course of the story. By turning the double perspective of science fantasy on the language in which she is telling the story, Elgin not only justifies the magic of names and word games that operates on Planet Ozark, but also reminds us of how belief in such magic originated in our own past. The humor arises from the fact that, thinking ourselves true believers in science, we retain our faith in linguistic magic.

All these stories work because both parent genres are ripe for a little mockery. Most science fiction stories and virtually all fantasies take themselves pretty seriously, and indeed both forms are capable of expressing pretty serious matters. Science fiction has a lot to say about the universe outside ourselves; fantasy about the inner one. But with repetition—repetition without thought—the impact of both genres wears off. By the fifth galactic empire, the ninth perilous quest, the dozenth parallel universe, all of those devices begin to seem rather shopworn.

The fantasy side, for example, suffers from its dependence on a limited stock of traditional images: wizards, dragons, unicorns, and the like. If a writer needs a little danger, a test for a hero, or a lesson in greed, it is easy—too easy—to trot out a dragon.

Then along comes science fantasy to rationalize dragons and thereby make them ridiculous. Looked at scientifically, dragons are too big to be graceful, too heavy to fly unless they are turned into blimp-like bags of gas, absurdly picky in their eating habits considering the available biomass of princesses. None of this invalidates the archetypal power of a well-imagined dragon: Smaug and Orm Embar remain awesome, soaring, crafty, ravenous marvels. But it may make it more difficult for a writer to use dragons without serious consideration of their significance to that writer.

The more formulaic fantasy is also limited to traditional story lines: the coming of age, the quest, the marriage of fairy and mortal, the apocalyptic battle. The problem with these narrative structures is that we know how they come out. Delay as long as she may, the fantasist must at last come to the foreordained ending. But the science fantasist need not. The narrative can skip out before the end, as Harold Shea does repeatedly, or it can simply refuse to follow the expected path, as the Ozark trilogy deftly avoids the romantic resolution it seems to be leading to. After reading these stories, we find that the traditional fantasies seem less predictable, their endings more precarious and therefore more affecting.

On the other side, one of the flaws of much science fiction is its overuse of the Robinson Crusoe hero—the man (it's almost always a man) who can survive anything, solve any problem singlehanded. He need only approach the problem with the proper scientific attitude and construct the relevant mechanism. This was a particular disease of the genre at the time that de Camp and Pratt created Harold Shea. Shea's self-image is in the scientific Robinson Crusoe mold, but the reality is quite different. He is least competent when most confident, and many of the problems he faces are simply beyond his abilities. When he does succeed, it is usually because of self-examination that reveals his own and consequently his enemies' internal weaknesses.

Science fantasy can derive humor from science, from magic, from the linguistic habits and beliefs that arise from those two perspectives, and from the storytelling formulas that make use of them. But the clash of rhetorics is not always funny. To quote Arthur Koestler again, "When two independent matrices of perception or reasoning interact with each other the result . . . is either a *collision* ending in laughter, or their *fusion* in a new intellectual synthesis, or their *confrontation* in an aesthetic experience" (*Act of Creation* 45). If the Harold Shea or Ozark stories illustrate some of the best use of comic "collision," science fantasies like Delany's *The Einstein Intersection* (1967) or Zelazny's *Creatures of Light and Darkness* (1969) are examples of creative "fusion," in which ancient myths are reinscribed in the language of scientific philosophy. Again, the effect of these stories is a product of their juxtaposition of two rhetorics, two ways of speaking about and, hence, of perceiving the fictional universe.

How did two rhetorical systems develop within one language in the first place? According to Owen Barfield, the split is older than what we think of as "science," yet it was not always present in human speech. The further back we trace the history of any word, says Barfield, the more concrete the meaning of that word seems to be. Thus, the ancestor of *spirit* was not an abstract essence or soul but a puff of wind. However, according to Barfield, it is a mistake to suppose that at some point the Indo-European-speaking tribes decided to apply the concrete term metaphorically to some principle of life within themselves. Instead, the older term meant something that was not exactly "wind" and not exactly "life" or "spirit" but a more inclusive category incorporating all of these. At some time in the past, there were no pure abstractions, as we can determine by finding the goad in *centrifugal* or the twist in *wrong*. Likewise, there were no purely concrete words. The words for "flame" or "seed" included in their meaning both the perceptible objects and the perceiver's subjective response. A more adequate translation might be something like "the flame I see dancing before me and the corresponding flame I perceive in myself."

Only later, as language and thought developed, did "these single meanings split up into contrasted pairs—the abstract and the concrete, particular and general, objective and subjective" (85). Until that time, says Barfield, natural symbol and spiritual significance were one and the same, and from that unity came myth:

> The naturalist is right when he connects the myth with the phenomena of nature, but wrong if he deduces it solely from these. The psycho-analyst is right when he connects the myth with "inner" (as we now call them) experiences, but wrong if he deduces it solely from these. Mythology is the ghost of concrete meaning. Connections between discrete phenomena, connections which are now apprehended as metaphor, were once perceived as immediate realities. (91–92)

In *Splintered Light: Logos and Language in Tolkien's World* (1983), Verlyn Flieger points out that J. R. R. Tolkien was an admirer of Barfield's work and aimed in his own writing at recapturing the undivided perception from which myth emerged. He certainly brought together the physical and the spiritual in such images as the binding Ring or Galadriel's prophetic Mirror, but only by limiting his treatment of physical reality to

a prescientific conception of the world. What the serious writer of science
fantasy is attempting to do is not to recapture an older worldview but to
forge a new one from elements that have long been developing in isolation.

Gods began appearing in science fantasy as early as 1913, in the
second installment of Burroughs's Mars series, which is titled *The Gods of
Mars*. Burroughs's way of reconciling the mythic perspective with the
scientific, however, is to discredit the former. The mythology of Mars,
with its mysterious River Iss in the Valley Dor, where the worthy dead go
to meet Issus, Goddess of Death, turns out to be a sham. Issus is a mad,
withered crone who feeds on those she is supposed to rule.

Once again, Burroughs established a formula on which later writers
continued to rely. The skeptical hero unmasking fraudulent gods reappears in pulp fantasy and science fantasy throughout the 1930s, '40s, and
'50s. Yet in the hands of Abraham Merritt, C. L. Moore, Leigh Brackett,
and Henry Kuttner, to name some of the most memorable utilizers of the
formula, something was added to it. The gods remain vindictive and
unworthy of the human worship they lay claim to, but they do begin to
represent something real. The forces they represent cannot be reduced to
trickery or scientific gadgetry; the gods can be defeated but at the loss of
some intangible value, which may be equated with the inward dimension
of which Barfield speaks.

By the 1960s, a number of writers reconsidered the formulaic demand
for the defeat of myth by science. Andre Norton, in particular, helped
forge a new formula in which the protagonist accepts and incorporates
within himself two kinds of truth, one scientific and the other magical. In
such novels as *Catseye* (1961), *The Beast Master* (1959), and *Judgment on
Janus* (1963), she creates a future history in which technology has led to
disaster, with whole planets destroyed by warfare among civilizations
with too much knowledge and too little wisdom. Within this context,
however, a few individuals learn to reject the mechanistic vision. Ac-
knowledging their kinship with the natural world, they gain the power to
defeat threats like the animated empty spacesuit of *Judgment*. This power
is usually represented as both outside and inside the hero: it is in one
sense a ancient godlike being and in another sense a hitherto untapped
human capacity.

Many writers made use of Norton's science fantasy formula, including
Marion Zimmer Bradley, Anne McCaffrey, and Ursula K. Le Guin. Despite Le Guin's self-criticism, quoted earlier, her first four novels mingle
the scientific and mythic perspectives with ever increasing conviction. In
Rocannon's World, Le Guin posits two cultures, one a space-going tech-
nocracy and the other a feudal society with a belief in magic. In her

prologue, a woman from the feudal society visits the world of the scientists, and in the novel proper the anthropologist Rocannon returns the favor. Both times, events are perceived according to the biases of the onlooker, either as straightforward cause and effect or as the workings-out of legend. The mix is largely successful and would be more so if, as Le Guin says, she had kept her science more rigorously scientific and her magic less eclectic. By the novel's end, Rocannon has come to view the natives' outlook as no less valid than his own: what he has been calling telepathy and coincidence might with equal justice be called magic and fate.

The contrast between high and low technologies, and the attempt to combine the truths accessible to each, reappears in Le Guin's *Planet of Exile* (1966), *City of Illusions* (1967), and *The Left Hand of Darkness* (1969). In the last of these, the narrative form itself reflects the fusion, for it alternates eyewitness reports by the alien envoy, Genly Ai, with the legends, tales, and songs of Gethenian natives. The story would not be complete without both kinds of narratives.

Roger Zelazny's science fantasies constitute a series of variations on the theme of technological advancement so great that men and women can become the gods they have always imagined. In *Lord of Light* (1967) the Hindu pantheon has been recreated on a colony planet, and in *Creatures of Light and Darkness* a more loosely interpreted Egyptian pantheon rules the entire universe. This formula serves Zelazny very well, allowing him to suggest that at the end of the road of scientific discovery lie the same problems our ancestors dreamed of. He implies that it is easier to acquire godhood than enlightenment.

A particularly ingenious way of juxtaposing the rational and emotional or scientific and magical perspectives is that utilized by Samuel Delany in *The Einstein Intersection*. In this novel, Delany finds the justification for looking beyond science within science itself. Citing the mathematician Goedel as a sort of patron saint of improbability, he constructs a world in which nothing is what it seems, and the old Einsteinian limits on perception and movement are bypassed. The characters in his novel, who seem to be mutated humans, are not human at all; rather, they are, as the computer PHAEDRA says to one, "a bunch of psychic manifestations, multi-sexed and incorporeal . . . trying to put on the limiting mask of humanity" (148). The ways these beings find order in their irrational world is to reenact human myths, from Orpheus to Billy the Kid.

Richard Cowper, in *The Road to Corlay* (1979) and two sequels, uses science fantasy to create a sort of post-Christian mythology with its roots in both faith and science. The quasi-medieval future depicted in Cowper's story is the result of a disaster caused by humans, a flood triggered by abuse of the environment:

> The Drowning was the direct result of humanity's corporate failure to see beyond the end of its own nose. By 1985 it was already quite obvious that the global climate had been modified to the point where the polar ice caps were affected. (55)

Few, however, remember the scientific explanation of the flood. To most people it was the Third Coming, a scourge sent by God to prepare the way for a spiritual rebirth at the beginning of the third millennium A.D. Though the immediate cause was man's technological overreaching, it also seems to represent divine intercession, fitting thus into a prophetic sequence: "The first coming was the man; the second was fire to burn him; the third was water to drown the fire, and the fourth is the Bird of Dawning" (38). After Christ comes Pentecost, then floods, and finally, at the time of the story, the White Bird.

This bird, like the flood, is a key image connecting the scientific and supernatural viewpoints. There is no visible, tangible bird in the story. It first appears as a vision, perhaps a mass hallucination, on New Year's Eve of the year 2999. The source of the vision is a tune played by a young piper, who is martyred immediately after. Thereafter, the White Bird is considered to manifest itself in various forms: in the pipes, in the tune the boy played, in the saint's legend that forms, in certain followers of the new faith, and in their developing psychic powers.

To the faithful, the bird is real and capable of miracles. However, Cowper is careful always to provide alternative explanations. The maker of the pipes, though he is called the Wizard of Bowness, may have performed his wizardry through rediscovered technology: "in Kendal the folk used to whisper that he'd stored up a treasurehouse of wisdom from the Old Times" (28). The pipes' magic could be explained as sonic manipulation of emotions. Other seemingly magical phenomena might be the result of a mutation for extrasensory perception and psi powers.

Reinforcing this view of events is a second plot concerning a man from our own time who, as a result of an experiment with "compound neurodrugs," finds himself inhabiting the body of a man a thousand years in the future. His experiences are witnessed by his coworkers on a sort of super electro-encephalograph hooked up to his unconscious body. He and the research team monitoring him interpret events scientifically, while the characters in the future see them from a religious or magical perspective. The former view assumes a rationally explainable, mechanistic universe, while the latter sees the world as a moral battleground in which immaterial forces may be embodied temporarily, as the White Bird is embodied in the piper and his tune.

Does Cowper reconcile the two views? His plot is so engineered that its resolution depends on both. The twentieth-century research team sends a man into the future. There he meets and falls in love with a woman who thus becomes the foretold Bride of Time; their child will carry on the work of the White Bird. Each event is both natural and magical, both wave and particle, as it were.

By overlapping the two kinds of narrative, Cowper is not so much attempting to reconcile scientific and religious worldviews as examining the nature of other kinds of nonmaterial entities—beliefs, ideas, perceptions—and showing how they impinge on the physical world in ways not yet predictable by science. Hence the emphasis on images of the real but intangible: the rush of invisible wings, a story that changes lives, and a tune that can heal or kill and overload a circuit a thousand years before it is played.

The past decade has produced many more varieties of science fantasy than can be examined here. Octavia Butler applies a scientific perspective to African myths in *Wild Seed* (1980). Her shape-shifting immortal Anyanwu passes to her children in both the old world and the new the ability to survive with integrity in the face of human oppression and supernatural threat. Because Anyanwu's abilities are based on self-knowledge, down to the chemical processes within her own cells, they cannot be taken away or misused even by the amoral Doro, whose powers of invasion and possession are in some senses the male equivalent of her female, generative ones. Butler shows how the cultural heritage of African Americans can provide understanding of the present and direction for the future, for Anyanwu's descendants will be the psychically gifted Patternists of Butler's other novels. The old concepts of mother goddess, werewolf, and *ogbanje*, or spirit child, become ways of comprehending the meaning and potential uses of genetic manipulation and other infant or unborn technologies.

In writing the four-volume *Book of the New Sun* (1980–83) and its sequel *The Urth of the New Sun* (1987), Gene Wolfe has demonstrated that science fantasy has as much potential for epic grandeur and symbolic complexity as either parent genre, which means as any form of fiction. Wolfe's imagined world easily accepts the discourse of either form, for it projects a time when advanced technology represents not the future but the distant past, traces of which remain and mingle with the magic that may be only technology more advanced still.

From vocabulary to overall narrative shape, Wolfe makes full use of science fantasy's double vision. He introduces the new and strange by using words that are old and strange: archaic, half-familiar words like *fuligin, lazaret, hierodule,* and *pelerine.* Mostly Latinate, these terms simultaneously suggest the Latin vocabulary of science and the Latin of medieval church, court, and coven. Wolfe generally invents by reusing what is forgotten: a mix of history, legend, and literary sources generates a narrative of seemingly inexhaustible fertility. Far-future Urth features scenes of horror, eerie beauty, decadence, rural simplicity, and sheer otherness that one can ascribe no human quality to.

But many of the most vivid inventions are the direct result of the science fiction-fantasy fusion. A creature of Arabic legend becomes the alzabo, a hyena-like creature that borrows the voices of its victims to tempt other prey. From the tissues of the alzabo, then, science has isolated a drug that enables humans to gain the memories of others—but only by imitating another legend and becoming ghouls. To take another example, a character named Jonas hides a secret: one of his arms is mechanical. But he is no ordinary science fiction cyborg. The mechanical arm and most of his body are original. A robot who has survived beyond the ability of his culture to repair him, he has been given an arm and head of flesh to replace damaged parts, and thereby turned into a tragic figure burdened by his partial humanity.

Wolfe's hero Severian must evolve into a savior of humankind, and his salvation involves the regeneration of earth's, or Urth's, sun. Every step of his task is mythic: his journey toward rulership; his two talismans, the executioner's sword and the healing jewel; his testing as representative of and intercessor for mankind; and his destruction and renewal of the earth. Every step also fits into the rhetorical pattern of science fiction, for each involves his learning another lost secret of the technological past and thereby gaining more control over his life. The New Sun itself loses none of its mystical, apocalyptic meaning for being fueled by a white hole. Within the narrative context, the leaking of energy into our universe through a white hole can be also a White Fountain, sign of the Increate's victory over entropy. Neither way of referring to it exhausts the reality of the thing itself, but both together provide a way of establishing its relationship to Severian and to ourselves.

These mythic science fantasies examine the twofold implications of words and images. In the best of these works, archetypes are subjected to the same scrutiny that a writer of conventional science fiction will give to the paradoxes of time travel or the ecological implications of terraforming new worlds. The test of good science fantasy is that it generate patterns we can respond to as we do to well-made fantasy without losing the cognitive dimension of good science fiction.

The comic science fantasies are not so ambitious, but they too make us more aware of the assumptions underlying science fiction and fantasy. They are particularly good at revealing the weaknesses inherent in both forms, the shoddy places in the fabric that serious writers in either genre are careful to camouflage.

Through humor, science fantasy reveals that the fantasist and the science fiction writer are often incomplete enchanters, the one out of touch with contemporary knowledge of the universe around us, the other unaware of the complex inner worlds of his characters. The first comic science fantasies don't go much beyond pointing out the faults of either form, but their joking collisions opened the way for more serious fusions and confrontations of the symbolic and the scientific. Those early de Camp and Pratt-falls led the way to narratives like Gene Wolfe's: mythic renderings of our scientific understanding and scientific examinations of our oldest beliefs.

EIGHT

Recapturing the Modern
World for the Imagination

WITHIN A GENRE LIKE FANTASY, subgenres regularly emerge, merge, or disintegrate. One such subgenre is science fantasy; another is the women's coming-of-age novel discussed in chapter 6. These subgenres, like the larger set of which they are a part, are fuzzy sets. They radiate from a few well-known and influential texts, as each new author construes the defining principles of those texts and adapts the perceived type to her own ends. A text that was conceived by its author as a development within one type of fantasy may serve subsequent writers as a model for quite a different variety, if its deviations from type are reinterpreted as a new set of norms. If a subgenre attracts enough interest from readers and writers, it may eventually change the center of gravity of the whole genre, with its own exemplary texts replacing the originals as the defining instances of the set, until the former norms begin to seem like divergences.

Of all the subgenres to emerge within fantasy in recent years, the one that promises to reshape the genre most significantly is as yet unnamed, or rather no name for it has proved adequate. Sometimes called "low fantasy" (Tymn 5), sometimes "real world fantasy" or "modern urban fantasy," it is characterized by the avoidance of the enclosed fantasy worlds predominant in earlier fantasies, from Lewis Carroll's Wonderland to Ursula K. Le Guin's Earthsea. Instead, these fantasies describe settings that seem to be real, familiar, present-day places, except that they contain the magical characters and impossible events of fantasy.

126

Fantasies of this sort are not really unprecedented. The Victorian writer F. Anstey exploited the comic possibilities of the eruption of magic into middle-class London in books such as *Vice Versa* (1882), and his lead was followed by the great Edwardian children's fantasist Edith Nesbit. Horror writers, likewise, have always made use of familiar settings: the gulfs of irrationality and violence that their stories open up derive their effectiveness from the apparent ordinariness and security that they breach. A third established use of the fantastic in realistic settings is to generate satirical parables, like Gogol's "The Nose."

Most closely related to the new form is the mode of writing called magic realism. Neither exclusively comic nor horrific, nor even satirical, magic realism calls on all of these responses as part of a larger structure. The term was borrowed from art criticism, since these stories often resemble the meticulously surreal paintings of René Magritte or Giorgio De Chirico. The magic realists of Latin America deliberately violate the norms of a realism associated with colonial powers and capitalist systems (Young and Hollaman 3). By placing magical beliefs on a par with science and blending legend with history, writers like Gabriel García Márquez, Julio Cortázar, Clarice Lispector, and María Luisa Bombal create fictional worlds at once solid and slippery. Fantastic beings move through real historical events; realistic characters undergo mysterious transformations; the foreground is starkly real but the background is obscured and deepened by veils of mist. Many magic realist texts have been both critical and popular successes because they combine inventive fertility, folktale-like plots, and a resistance to interpretive closure: features characteristic of at least one form of literary postmodernism, as discussed in chapter 3.

The Latin American form of magic realism has influenced many North American writers, not only among "literary" or "writing school" fictionalists but also within genres like science fiction and fantasy. Though *One Hundred Years of Solitude* (1968) might seem to have very little in common with *The Lord of the Rings* (besides length), the fantasy genre as it had evolved in the 1960s and '70s was well prepared to integrate the influence of magic realism, since writers like Le Guin, Alan Garner, and Roger Zelazny had already begun to explore the capacity of the fantasy form to compound narrative complexity and confound expectations without violating generic rules. Thus, it is sometimes difficult to tell which contemporary fantasies are deliberate evocations of postmodernist uncertainty and which are accidental reinventions by ingenious exploiters of formula. I suspect some of the texts that I have most enjoyed are, one might say, knowingly naive, while others are naively wise. In either case, the traditions and constraints of the fantasy genre seem to work to prevent the kind of archness that dooms John Updike's *The Witches of Eastwick*

(1984) or the formlessness that overtakes Stephen Millhauser's otherwise promising *From the Realm of Morpheus* (1986).

The magic realist example has worked to reinforce fantasy's move from other-worldly to "real world" settings. Replacing Poictesme or Narnia with Ann Arbor or Seattle is not a simple matter of changing the names and descriptions. Fantasies such as R. A. MacAvoy's *Tea with the Black Dragon* (1983), Eleanor Arnason's *Daughter of the Bear King* (1987), Orson Scott Card's *Seventh Son* (1987), or Nancy Willard's *Things Invisible to See* (1985) create and resolve contradictions in such a way as to challenge our notions about the ways literature can transform experience and about the limitations of fantasy as a genre.

Realistic modes of fiction attempt to generate, as a primary response, *recognition*. If a novel like *Huckleberry Finn* succeeds, we feel we have been given an authentic glimpse into the human condition, at least as manifest in a particular time and place. Fantasy, though, as I argued earlier, is directed primarily toward a kind of response we call *wonder*. Wonder is connected with seeing things not so much as they are but as they might be or ought to be. The unknown can generate wonder; so can the familiar seen in a new light. (In identifying the primary response, I do not wish to suggest that realistic writing cannot generate its own form of wonder—consider Huck Finn's experiences on the river—or that fantasy might not also hold up a mirror to human nature.)

The ability of fantasy to generate wonder, as I suggested in chapter 1, is closely tied to both setting and story line. The *setting* is traditionally an enclosed Other World of magical beings and miraculous events: Narnia or Middle Earth. The *story* follows the fairy tale model: whatever happens along the way, the ending will come out right. We sometimes call this coming out right a happy ending, for short, but readers of the great fantasies know it is much more ambiguous and less trivial than that.

The setting makes the ending possible. A magical world cannot be confused with real life, and so the story is entitled to reach the most satisfying, rather than the most probable, conclusion. Frodo will reach Mount Doom and destroy the Ring. The conclusion, in turn, validates our response to the imagined world, our astonished delight at ents and elves and mallorn trees. A different ending might have reinforced experiences in Saruman's tower or Shelob's lair; it might have generated irony or horror, but not wonder.

But the recent fantasies mentioned above, and others by Megan Lindholm, Charles de Lint, Sheri S. Tepper, Diana Paxson, Emma Bull, Peter Beagle, and John Crowley, paradoxically attempt to reattach the wonder-generating mechanisms of fantasy to realistic-seeming settings and situations.

At this point I must settle on a name for this subgenre of fantasy, so I don't have to keep listing authors or titles. "Magic realism" has too many other applications; "low fantasy" implies a judgment with which I do not agree; "'real world' fantasy" requires either laying in a large stock of quotation marks or seeming to take for granted the nature of reality. One might borrow a name from the past, naming the form after one of its precursors: Nesbittian or Charles Williamsesque fantasy. But instead of any of these, I am going to suggest the name *indigenous fantasy*. That is to say, this is fantasy that is, like an indigenous species, adapted to and reflective of its native environment.

The choice to write indigenous rather than Tolkienian fantasy involves making two simultaneous and incompatible assertions: first, that the story takes place in the ordinary world accessible to our senses, and, second, that this world contains—contrary to all sensory evidence and experience—magical beings, supernatural forces, and a balancing principle that makes fairy tale endings not only possible but obligatory.

Indigenous fantasy is thus an inherently problematic form. It is also, by the same token, inherently interesting, for one wonders what strategies the author will adopt to conceal or bridge the built-in conceptual gap. The gap itself reflects our different ways of knowing and responding to the world, the magical and scientific dimensions of thought and language that are reflected in science fantasy. It also reflects the less evident gulf between story and history, our two ways of organizing time and placing ourselves within it.

The most rigorously realistic fiction emulates history in all its muddle and sprawl. Its mode of discourse is essentially reportorial, for history ultimately derives from the eyewitness account. We make use of that discourse every day in conversation, telling what we saw, what we did, what someone said to us. We usually make an attempt to arrange our account in chronological order, with the logical sequence of cause and effect providing the connections between events: "Then he got noisy again, so I hit him with the lamp."

So long as one sticks to the rules—tell what happened or reasonably might have happened, describe what one saw or might have seen, keep events more or less in order and causes evident—one can incorporate any incident or emotion, adopt any perspective or style. This kind of reporting is so adaptable and seems so natural that we tend to forget that it is not the only form of discourse available, even in conversation. There are also, for instance, tall tales and jokes, neither of which is arranged according to the rules of historical discourse. Fantasy shares with these other oral genres a certain contrived or constructed quality. Its characters are chosen and its incidents arranged to fit a predetermined pattern, which allows for the achievement of a particular effect: laughter in the case of the joke, the refreshment of vision called wonder in the case of the fantasy.

Defining serious literature only in terms of the discourse of reporting, as critics have done for the past century, ignores the human need to cast the events of one's life in story form, rather than exclusively in reference to history. Stories have heroes, whereas histories only have actors. Stories have beginnings and ends, and an internal dynamic that moves them toward a particular goal. The form of a story is its chief meaning, whereas the meaning of history must be inferred through application to external values.

Other World fantasy more or less bypasses history by inventing a setting in which every object, incident, or motivation may be assumed to be in service to a preordained and comprehensible narrative pattern. The first hint the fictional world is not intended to stand for the world of experience tells us that we are not in reportorial mode, but in some other form of discourse in which chronology may be violated; in which causality is less important than teleology—the direction things are headed; and in which characters are defined primarily by their roles in bringing the story to its conclusion and only secondarily by their individual traits and interactions.

There was a time when this division, between story and history, did not exist or seemed unimportant. Italo Calvino has written a plausible reconstruction of origins of the earliest recorded magical narrative, which we usually call myth. He points out that the elements of a myth are the everyday realities in the life of what he calls the "tribal storyteller." Hypothesizing a South American background, though any other would do, he mentions jaguars and toucans as typical actors, chess pieces for the game of story. For possible actions, we might have hunting, flying, eating, drinking, mating, and dying—assuming only the jaguar and toucan as sources of inspiration. Then what Calvino calls the "combinatorial game" begins. Jaguar hunts, toucan flies, she-jaguar meets he-jaguar, toucan flies too close and dies. The storyteller gets bolder: toucan tries hunting, jaguar learns to fly, dead she-jaguar returns to haunt he-jaguar. The magic which is narrative possibility takes these simple facts and transforms them until eventually the teller achieves a narrative symmetry which is recognized by his listeners. They, then, are compelled to retell that particular story, refining it further, until it becomes what we call a myth.

The modern storyteller likewise can assemble actors and events and attempt to combine them into myth, but two key ingredients from Calvino's mythmaking scenario are lacking. One is the context in which storytelling could spill over into ritual and belief. The other, which is related to the first, is the availability of a whole set of game pieces without which the game lacks a level of combinatorial possibility.

The tribal storyteller's world included jaguar and toucan, and so he could readily transform their movements and attributes into narrative. But Calvino does not mention that the storyteller's world also included ghosts, walking trees, and ancestors who were both jaguar and human. These things were also parts of reality: ghosts looked a certain way, spoke a certain way. The storyteller knew: he had seen them. These elements did more than merely add to the storyteller's repertoire. They transformed everything else within it.

A simple tale was likely to explode "into a terrible revelation," as Calvino says (79), because toucan and jaguar and storyteller and listener were already connected in a web of kinship and transformation and magic, a web that was known through the stories but extended well beyond their boundaries.

Combining the familiar with the magical, which was also familiar, the tribal storyteller created a mythic discourse. The writer of indigenous fantasy is attempting to recreate that discourse from two now sundered sources. The magical web is no longer part of the discourse of everyday reality, and so our novels and histories do not explode so easily into myth. But the discourse of magic, which is roped off into fantasy worlds, has lost something as well.

The great advantage of the discourse of reporting is its property of extension. Once we know we are in a story in reportorial mode, we can extend the narrator's observations in any direction. If the story mentions London, we can assume Paris. We can fill in Tower Bridge and the dome of St. Paul's, whether or not they are invoked specifically. We can supply Henry VIII and Victoria, Samuel Johnson and Virginia Woolf. Even the least well-read can provide traffic and parks and shops and cinemas to fill in the background of what the narrator actually chooses to notice. Ultimately the world of the story extends in an unbroken path to the reader's own doorstep. Thus the reader does a lot of the hard work of bringing a story to life.

Occasionally, of course, our observations and the narrator's will fail to agree, but generally we can set these lapses aside. If snakes are described as slimy or Boise as east of Butte, we can blame authorial ignorance or narrator's unreliability and assume the rest of the fictional world corresponds point for point with our own models of reality.

What if, however, the narrator speaks of clouds colliding overhead, or describes a troupe of tiny people hoisting sail in a bathtub. The link with our own surroundings is broken: there is no continuous path from such a scene to our own space. We are forced to interpret such descriptions as statements in another mode of discourse: metaphors, perhaps, in a metaphysical poem, or hallucinations that will be disavowed later in the narrative, or metafictional trickery. If no such explanation works, then these sorts of incidents force our reidentification of the whole narrative into the discourse of the wonder tale or fantasy.

Once that identification is made, the principle of extension ceases to operate. No longer can we be sure that the fictional London is situated across the Channel from a fictional Paris or that its history matches any part of the history we know. We know nothing for certain until the narrator tells us it is so. Is the sky blue? Is the world round? Perhaps, but don't bet on it.

Yet the reader needs some way of filling in at least an approximation of the story's background, so that each item named does not emerge from empty space. Otherwise the storyteller's discourse will be overburdened with naming:

> A man sat under a tree. The man was bilaterally symmetrical, made of flesh and blood, about six feet tall, with hair on one end and boots on the other. The tree was green-leafed and grey-barked. It could not speak. "Under" means touching the ground, in the direction of gravity's pull.

It is impossible—everything specified calls for further specification, so that no story could ever advance beyond its beginning point.

This is the reason that so many fantasies suffer from a certain thinness even while they seem to be overdetermined. Most fantasy worlds are radically reduced from the richness of actual experience.

What a fantasist can do to compensate is direct readers to a storytelling tradition for filling in inessential background. Although fairy tales are radically discontinuous with history, they are in a sense continuous with other fairy tales. As a way of filling in the empty fictional space, narrators refer the reader to the European fairy tale and romance tradition. Instead of an absolute void to mark off as best they can, many storytellers settle for a familiar and coherent landscape in which clouds *can* possibly clash and fairies go sailing. In most cases this is essentially a simplified version of the Middle Ages. Writers are attempting to rehistoricize fantastic assertions by placing them within an approximation of the most accessible milieu in which such statements could have been made within the discourse of reporting. Unfortunately, most contemporary fantasists lack the depth of antiquarian knowledge that allowed Tolkien or Morris to roam freely in a reconstructed medieval world. Nor do most fantasists, especially in America, have access to locales where fairy tale and legend are still a part of local culture, as they are in Alan Garner's Cheshire or Susan Cooper's Thames Valley.

For these reasons, borrowing a milieu from old stories is likely to result in settings that seem flimsy and flat, like cardboard stage sets. Yet, on the other hand, the magical web of relations that justifies a fairy tale's happy ending cannot be supported in a realistic narrative: it dissolves into coincidence and authorial intervention. The more carefully a writer shapes a narrative in historical mode, the more improbable it becomes.

In a fantastic tale, the deck is allowed—is even required—to be stacked in favor of the hero, for that is a hero's narrative function. The realistically conceived protagonist, though, has no such dispensation, and any sign of predisposition in his favor registers as sentimentality. An engineered resolution would imply that the story's outcome, like its characters and setting, derives from the real world, that the universe is ready to step in on the side of good, and we are no longer prepared to accept such a claim.

Yet a number of writers have attempted to find ways of combining—or rather recombining—these two types of discourse. Using American settings in which the mythic fusion of magic and everyday life does not linger even in memory, they have attempted to recapture the medieval or tribal storyteller's ability to feed observation into fantasy. Those who have succeeded have constructed narratives in which the inevitable falling-into-place of fantasy governs a world that seems continuous with the reader's experience.

Megan Lindholm's *Wizard of the Pigeons* (1986) illustrates the process. Like many writers of indigenous fantasy, Lindholm wrote Other World stories first and then turned to materials closer to hand, to try to integrate scenes and incidents from her hometown of Seattle, Washington, into a wonder tale.

To do so, she had to find a way of convincing readers that her Seattle is indeed the contemporary West Coast city they have seen or read about and at the same time a fantasy world in which impossible events demonstrate a secret and wondrous order, which will govern the course of the tale.

The wizard of the title is a street person. He is one of those people with too many layers of clothing, who launch into improbable conversations with strangers or with the empty air, who make us uncomfortable without threatening us, so that our usual response is to avert our eyes and walk past. In that averting of eyes is the rationale for making such a claim. Why can't an invisible person be doing impossible things? If we were to see him, for once, and, more importantly, to see what he sees, he could indeed be a wizard, and the area of Seattle marked by the boundaries of the public transit Ride Free Zone a fairyland.

What Lindholm must do is encourage the reader to accept Wizard's view of things (his role is also his name). He must not be merely derelict or incompetent, and so the vagaries of his behavior are presented in such a way that they seem in harmony with his surroundings:

> On such a day the cries of the gulls seem to drown out the traffic noises, and the fresh salt breath of the ocean is stronger than the exhaust of the passing cars. . . . The possibilities of the day tugged at Wizard's mind like a kite tugs on a string. So, although he had been standing for some time at a bus stop, when the bus finally came snorting into sight, he wandered away from the other passengers, letting his feet follow their own inclination. (2)

The description helps validate the point of view. Only after we have shared Wizard's pleasure in the bright October sunshine and listened to his internal guided tour of historic Seattle are we confronted by evidence that his thinking processes might be a little askew. Wizard has dropped into a curiosity shop to visit a friend:

> "So how's it going, old man?" Wizard greeted him softly.
> Sylvester gave a dry cough and began, "It was a hot and dusty day . . ."
> Wizard listened, politely nodding. It was the only story Sylvester had to tell, and Wizard was one of the few who could hear it. (3)

Sylvester is a mummy, "one of the best naturally preserved mummies existent in the western United States. It said so right on the placard beside his display case" (4).

Although we have doubts about a man who talks to mummies—and listens to them—the narrator counters our doubts with the idea that there is an unrecorded truth behind historical documentation. The pamphlets accompanying the display

> told everything there was to know, except who he had been, and why he had died in the sandy wastes from a bullet wound. And those secrets were the ones he whispered to Wizard, speaking in a voice as dry and dusty as his unmarked grave had been, in words so soft they barely passed the glass that separated them. (4)

In this way, Lindholm establishes that Wizard is not merely an eccentric having delusions. He is somehow more in touch with both the physical presence and the historical background of the mummy than are either the writers of the pamphlets or the conventional people who glance into the shop. His life on the streets justifies a cockeyed perspective on what is or is not physically possible, thereby bringing the discourse of the fantastic into play. At the same time, it also allows the narrator to lay claim to the chief validating mechanisms of realistic discourse: detailed description and reference to history. Wizard's special insight into history is translated into the discourse of fantasy when it is understood that its source is his receptiveness to the mummy's *story*: its transformation of mere event into a ritualized narrative directed toward an already known end.

From this encounter, the story moves toward more explicitly fantastic events, but always within the limits of Wizard's lifestyle and point of view. A mechanical gypsy in the curiosity shop slips Wizard a warning on a Tarot card. We learn about Wizard's special gift, which is to have things come to him unbidden. Knowledge of a stranger's affairs is simply there when he needs it, just as clothing, food, shelter, and sometimes small change make themselves available:

> He had found a box of tea bags in the dumpster in the alley behind the health food store. The corner of the box was crushed, but the tea bags were intact in their brightly colored envelopes. . . . In a dumpster four blocks away, he had found two packets of tall candles, each broken in several places, but still quite useful. An excellent morning. The magic was flowing today, and the light was still before him. (13)

Details that could be arranged into a sociological study of the homeless here contribute to the fantasy because they are interpreted as magical, which is to say as Wizard's power and fate working in tandem.

Wizard meets other wizards: Rasputin, Euripides, and the most powerful, Cassie. Cassie comes and goes through many Seattles, leading Wizard through doors that weren't there before she appeared, into the past or the city that might have been had there been no fire at the turn of the century. She never looks the same twice. Lindholm takes evident pleasure in describing in great detail the physical appearance that would define and restrict Cassie in a realistic narrative, but here tells us only that we don't know Cassie's limits.

Cassie is, in a sense, the discourse of the fantastic itself. She is the one who explains the art of wizardry to Wizard, and her explanations always take the form of stories. She draws part of her power from children's rhymes, the simple narratives to which little girls jump rope. She is known to the reader primarily through her stories and through her role in this story, which is the one who tells truths the listener is not prepared to understand. She is both fictional and metafictional. After telling one vivid story about the bombing of Norwich, she is asked by Wizard if she was really there at the beginning of World War II. Her answer is, "That story is always told in the first person" (74).

With these clues before us, by the midpoint of the book we are able to spot Cassie in a rapid succession of guises. We recognize the battered vagrant, the neat white-haired woman, the short curly-haired Jewish woman, the stout little black woman, the slender Polynesian, the young student, simply because any person appearing at those moments, saying the kinds of things they are saying, *has* to be Cassie.

Through Cassie's stories and Wizard's gifts, we come to see the city of Seattle, its physical presence and its history, as fully encompassed by the magical tale. Even poverty, prostitution, and violence can enter into the ordering mechanism of story, as Wizard exercises his power to heal victims of these urban diseases.

Wizard's own story involves learning to control the relationship of present and past. His past is dominated by violence and despair: he was a sniper in Vietnam, possibly a prisoner of the Vietcong. At one point in the book that past threatens to reemerge and define him not as Wizard but as Mitchell Ignatius Reilly, emotionally maimed veteran. As long as that is the only past he possesses, he can only function by cutting it off, keeping the documents that would tie him to it locked away in a box in a trunk in an attic of the deserted building he has made his home. But the past still lurks, unacknowledged. The box marked with his initials becomes a focus for evil: the residue of evil from the war, the many small evils of urban life, the evil impulses that he has been trained to make use of as a soldier. All of these coalesce in a gray presence called MIR.

Wizard can defeat MIR neither by denying the past nor by resuming his old identity. He must find a new identity, which involves crossing over to a new narrative line. Instead of being Mitch Reilly, whose past is unbearable and whose future is hopeless, he must find a past and future for Wizard. Here Cassie can help, for her stories hold many pasts. All he needs to do is find a story, like the one of the bombing of Norwich, that can be told in the first person, or rather that *he* can tell, truthfully, in the first person.

MIR tries to impose a story on Wizard. It throws him into a memory, a narrative about young boys killing a pet black rooster and at the same time learning a lesson in violence and indifference to cruelty. The only question is whose memory it is: which of the boys was Wizard?

But that question is a trap. Cassie shows Wizard how to break the chain of cause and effect and turn realistic narrative into magical. "I remembered being all those boys, as soon as the grayness showed them to me," says Wizard. "Yet having seen them I would not choose to have been any of them."

"Don't you see?" responds Cassie. "You were there, yes. But you were the Black Rooster" (75).

If Wizard could have been the Black Rooster, he could have had other lives as well. One story Cassie gives him early in the novel provides a particularly useful past if the identity he is looking for is that of a magic-maker and hero. It is about a young girl and an old man robed in blue who teaches her about herbs and magic. Wizard does not recognize himself in the story—he even makes fun of it: "And the old man was Merlin, and the little girl was Cassie. The End" (63). But the little girl *was* Cassie, and the old man may have been Merlin but was certainly Wizard, and it isn't the End.

When he learns that his true past lies in stories, Wizard is freed to fight MIR in the present, and his own narrative can hook up with the happy ending appropriate to a fairy tale. The episode of the Vietnam War, like that of the Black Rooster, is safely encapsulated as an episode, a necessary trial along the way, instead of an open-ended nightmare. The past can be harrowing so long as the whole has a purpose and a resolution.

Lindholm has constructed a narrative that says, by its very shape, that telling magical tales may be a way of taking control of an otherwise unmanageable reality. Other writers of indigenous fantasy similarly describe how the fantastic mode can take possession of realistic discourse, utilizing narrative strategies comparable to Lindholm's filtering reality through the eyes of an urban scavenger.

As a result, these stories share a particular concreteness that is the farthest thing from the vague settings of purely derivative fantasy. Lindholm's Seattle, Peter Beagle's Berkeley, Emma Bull's Minneapolis, and Nancy Willard's Ann Arbor provide firm ground and vivid detail to the narratives, a familiar phenomenon in autobiography or local-color writing, but rather new to fantasy. One can feel the author's relish in placing magical incidents on real street corners and turning acquaintances into fairies and mages.

The point of view character in most of these fantasies is in some way marginal, not among those who are authorized to make judgments about what is real or appropriate. Sheri S. Tepper and Eleanor Arnason use a woman's perspective, Orson Scott Card and Nancy Willard use a child's, Diana Paxson and Peter Beagle draw on the medieval revival movement, and Emma Bull and R. A. MacAvoy make musicians serve as representatives of those whose needs and interests are not served by consensus reality. What is required seems to be a perspective close enough to common sense to allow for a sense of continuity with the reader's world but at the same time open to impossible events and miraculous explanations. We may not believe, for instance, that Wizard's magic brings him quarters when he craves coffee or enables him to feed pigeons out of an inexhaustible bag of popcorn, but we believe someone like Wizard could believe it, and his receptiveness allows our temporary acquiescence.

The transitional point of view, however, need not be that of a true believer in the supernatural. It just has to be someone who can, like Wizard, *tell* the magical tale to us. In a curious way, John Crowley is able to use Smoky Barnable's skepticism to allay our own in *Little, Big,* and to generate through Smoky's perceptions a whole anthology of modes of discourse. At the same time, Smoky allows the reader to make use of that sense of continuity from which realistic narratives derive so much of their solidity.

Smoky is a sort of displaced person in the twentieth century. Educated by his father,

> at sixteen, Smoky knew Latin, classical and medieval; Greek; some old-fashioned mathematics; and he could play the violin a little. He had smelled few books other than his father's leather-bound classics; he could recite two hundred lines of Virgil more or less accurately; and he wrote in a perfect Chancery hand. (6)

This education has effectively isolated Smoky, just as Wizard's war experience cut him off from the concerns of the ordinary residents of Seattle. Smoky, with no marketable skills, a very imperfect knowledge of current events, and no confidence in his own ability to make judgments about reality, is ready to be drawn into a group whose view of the world is, if odd, at least secure. This is the Drinkwater family. They maintain a set of beliefs dating from the middle of the last century, the age of spirit rapping, reincarnation, and photographs of the fairies.

Marriage to Alice Drinkwater brings Smoky into the midst of a colony of heirs to the great nineteenth-century wave of spiritualist frenzy, now isolated but still thriving like sea creatures in a tide pool. His marriage also brings Smoky in contact with a number of eccentric and fantastic forms of narrative discourse, which help thicken the texture of the magic tale by giving us more ways to pour our own experiences into it.

We can credit the style of the book's opening to Smoky's upbringing. This is how he would introduce himself, drawing on those leather-bound volumes of his childhood:

> On a certain day in June, 19—, a young man was making his way on foot northward from the great City to a town or place called Edgewood, that he had been told of but had never visited. (3)

Though the City is obviously New York and the unspecified date sometime in the 1960s, Smoky never really lives in that setting, for it does not fit the language he has for describing reality. The only connection he establishes there is with George Mouse, a Drinkwater cousin, and the quality of their relationship is conveyed through Smoky's peculiar vocabulary: "by then he and Smoky had become, as only Smoky in the whole world it seemed could any longer say with all seriousness, fast friends" (9).

Through George, Smoky meets Alice, and soon thereafter starts his journey to Edgewood, a place where an expression like "fast friends" is the least extraordinary sort of utterance. One of the pleasures in reading *Little, Big* is to trace the models from which the language of Edgewood is compounded, from *Winnie the Pooh* to Madame Blavatsky to *Little Nemo in Slumberland*.

Smoky's language is so much at home in this place that he is willing to suspend judgment on the parts of Edgewood that do not fit his notions of reality, such as talking animals:

"You said someone told you . . ."
"Spark," she said. "Or someone like him."
She looked closely at him, and he tried to compose his features into a semblance of pleasant attention. "Spark is the dog," he said. (15)

Once established at Edgewood, Smoky is surrounded by odd and old-fashioned narratives, such as Dr. Drinkwater's children's books, Great-Aunt Cloud's Tarot readings, Sophie's recountings of her dreams, and Great-Grandfather John Drinkwater's theosophical musings, with which the later editions of his architecture books were encrusted. Smoky never realizes that these narrating voices surrounding him are all speaking literal truth and all of a piece. Even though Smoky never really understands or believes, however, he is content to *make* believe. His stance—bemused, delighted, accepting without entirely trusting—is the reader's. Then, starting from that acquiescence, the reader finds the intertwining discourses of Edgewood reaching out to encompass other places and times, even the great City. History is engulfed by story, as it was once before, in the Middle Ages, when a historical figure like Emperor Frederick Barbarossa could find his way into the legend of the sleeping king under the mountain. As if to show the similarity, Crowley brings Barbarossa out of his sleep and into *this* story as well.

Smoky's son Auberon Barnable also brings the reader in contact with a more contemporary kind of history. During his stay in the City, Auberon becomes for a time a scavenger much like Lindholm's Wizard:

He had thrown himself on the City's mercy, and found that, like a strict mistress, she was kind to those who submitted utterly, held nothing back. By degrees he learned to do that; he who had always been fastidious . . . grew filthy, City dirt worked itself into his fabric ineradicably . . . . By autumn his knapsack was a useless rag, a cerement, and anyway had ceased to be large enough to hold a life lived on the streets; so like the rest of the secret City's epopts he carried paper shopping bags, one inside the other for strength, advertising in his degraded person many great establishments in turn. (379)

In this description, with its precise and arcane vocabulary, we can hear Auberon's self-dramatization, and behind that the accents of his father and teacher Smoky. Though Auberon's period of dereliction is only episode one among many, it serves here the same function as Wizard's cutting loose from conventionality: it makes the impossible seem only unexpected, and no more unexpected at that than any of the meetings and acquisitions in a wholly unplanned life.

Auberon passes through his derelict stage and goes home, but like Wizard he has had the course of his life changed. He is now ready to take up his role in the story, and it is at this point that he is given *his* new name and fabulous past. He finds out for the first time, for instance, that his City misadventure, triggered by the disappearance of his lover Sylvie, was engineered by supernatural beings. They are the same supernatural beings, indeed, who turned his great-grandfather August Drinkwater into a trout, another new fact in a now unpredictable past. Auberon is given both facts by an evidently reliable source, the trout itself, who promises that there will be a gift in compensation for Auberon's woes. Crowley wonderfully captures the fishy and prophetic discourse of its thoughts:

> Grandfather Trout's was not an affectionate soul, not now, not after all these years; but this was after spring, and the boy was after all flesh of his flesh, or so they said. He hoped anyway that if there *was* a gift in it, it wouldn't be one that would cause the boy any great suffering. (412)

Eventually Auberon becomes fully a function of the story, a fantastic being, Oberon to Sylvie's Titania. Other characters are similarly *narratized*. Their realistic attributes are simplified and intensified until they become pure narrative movements, which is to say mythic beings. Only Smoky retains the complexities and doubts that make him a realistic character, that keep him just on the threshold of the world of Faery, where he can look but not enter, neither believing nor disbelieving. He must stay in that halfway state if he is to continue to bridge the many sorts of discourse and thereby let *us* part way into the plot:

> . . . Smoky was willing, willing to take on this task, to take exception to none of it, to live his life for the convenience of others in whom he had never even quite believed, and spend his substance bringing about the end of a Tale in which he did not figure. (531)

The substance Smoky has to spend is, in a sense, his discourse, which holds together so many strands of language and plot. The "others" whose convenience he has served are ourselves, the audience, as well as the unseen troupe of fairies. As to the last clause above, he does, of course, figure in the Tale, for it has become his Tale even more than it is the Drinkwater family's, at least from our perspective.

When the story is all worked out, everyone dead or vanished or transformed, and even Smoky no longer there to anchor the fairy tale in reality, the narrative concludes with a passage of essentially realistic, though lyrical, discourse, as a way of showing what has vanished:

> It was anyway all a long time ago; the world, we know now, is as it is and not different; if there was ever a time where there were passages, doors, the borders open and many a crossing, that time is not now. The world is older than it was. Even the weather isn't as we remember it clearly once being; never lately does there come a summer day such as we remember, never clouds as white as that, never grass as odorous or shade as deep and full of promise as we remember they can be, as once upon a time they were. (538)

The real world, "as it is and not different," says Crowley's narrative, is empty without the world "once upon a time" that comes into being only in story. New York is no place unless it is also the City, teeming with elegance and vice and with all the stories into which those temptations can lead young heroes. The countryside, too, needs its stories, like Smoky's getting lost in the woods and meeting Mother Nature, whom he takes, not wrongly, for a neighbor of the Drinkwaters'. It needs Smoky's honeymoon in the moonlight on an island in a lake, and Alice's walking backward into a rainbow. These stories transform the world so that it is never without wonder: even Crowley's lament for lost beauty creates the image of that beauty.

It is unlikely that any of the indigenous fantasists intend readers to begin living like Wizard or expecting the fairies to bring about a transformation in their lives. When you convert history into story, you end up with precisely and only that—a story. Yet stories, by being different from nature or history, make nature accessible and history meaningful.

Fantasy, by its structure, emphasizes the difference between fiction and life, a difference which our critical tradition seemed for a long time to be determined to erase. Indigenous fantasy shows that fiction and life are not only separate but complementary. Those eccentric viewpoints sought by fantasists as a way of justifying divergence from the strictly representational are probably as useful to the writer as to the reader. They are enabling mechanisms, ways of evading the rational censor, so that our own tribal storytellers can resume their proper function, reclaim their unique discourse, and recapture the modern world for the imagination.

Works Cited

Abel, Elizabeth, Marianne Hirsch, and Elizabeth Langland, eds. *The Voyage In: Fictions of Female Development.* Hanover: UP of New England, 1983.
Alexander, Lloyd. *The Black Cauldron.* New York: Holt, 1965.
———. *The Book of Three.* New York: Holt, 1964.
———. *The Castle of Llyr.* New York: Holt, 1966.
———. *The High King.* New York: Holt, 1968.
———. *Taran Wanderer.* New York: Holt, 1967.
Anstey, F. (Thomas Anstey Guthrie). *Vice Versa.* London: Murray, 1882.
Arnason, Eleanor. *Daughter of the Bear King.* New York: Avon, 1987.
Attebery, Brian. *The Fantasy Tradition in American Literature: From Irving to Le Guin.* Bloomington: Indiana UP, 1980.
Auerbach, Erich. *Mimesis: The Representation of Reality in Western Literature.* Trans. Willard Trask. Princeton: Princeton UP, 1953.
Baldwin, Karen. "Family Narratives as First Memories of Childhood." Conference paper, American Folklore Society. San Diego, CA, 13 October 1984.
Barfield, Owen. *Poetic Diction: A Study in Meaning.* 2d ed., rpt. with an introduction by Howard Nemerov. New York: McGraw-Hill, 1964.
Barth, John. *Chimera.* New York: Random, 1972.
———. "The Literature of Exhaustion." *The Atlantic* August 1967: 29–34.
———. "The Literature of Replenishment." *The Atlantic* January 1980: 65–71.
Beagle, Peter. *The Folk of the Air.* New York: Ballantine, 1986.
Bleiler, E. F., ed. *Supernatural Fiction Writers: Fantasy and Horror.* 2 vols. New York: Scribner's, 1985.
Borges, Jorge Luis. "Pierre Menard, Author of the Quixote." *Labyrinths.* Trans. James E. Irby. New York: New Directions, 1962. Rpt. in *Fantastic Worlds: Myths, Tales, and Stories.* Ed. Eric S. Rabkin. New York: Oxford UP, 1979. 415–23.
Bradley, Marion Zimmer. *The World Wreckers.* Boston: Gregg, 1979.
Brooke-Rose, Christine. *A Rhetoric of the Unreal: Studies in Narrative and Structure, Especially of the Fantastic.* Cambridge: Cambridge UP, 1981.
Brown, Fredric. *Angels and Spaceships.* New York: Dutton, 1954.
Brownstein, Rachel M. *Becoming a Heroine: Reading about Women in Novels.* New York: Viking, 1982.
Bull, Emma. *War for the Oaks.* New York: Ace, 1987.
Burroughs, Edgar Rice. *The Gods of Mars.* All-Story, 1913; rpt. Chicago: McClurg, 1918.
———. *A Princess of Mars.* All-Story, 1912, as "Under the Moons of Mars"; rpt. Chicago: McClurg, 1917.
Butler, Octavia E. *Wild Seed.* Garden City: Doubleday, 1980.
Calvino, Italo. *The Castle of Crossed Destinies.* Trans. William Weaver. New York: Harcourt, 1977.

———. *Cosmicomics*. Trans. William Weaver. New York: Harcourt, 1968.

———. "Myth in the Narrative." Trans. Erica Freiberg. In *Surfiction: Fiction Now . . . and Tomorrow*. Ed. Raymond Federman. Chicago: Swallow, 1975. 75–81.

Card, Orson Scott. *Seventh Son*. New York: TOR, 1987.

Carpenter, Humphrey. *J.R.R. Tolkien: A Biography*. Boston: Houghton, 1977.

Cawelti, John. *Adventure, Mystery, and Romance: Formula Stories and Popular Culture*. Chicago: U of Chicago P, 1976.

Chatman, Seymour. *Story and Discourse: Narrative Structure in Fiction and Film*. Ithaca: Cornell UP, 1978.

Clifton, Michael. "Jewels of Wonder, Instruments of Delight: Science Fiction, Fantasy, and Science Fantasy as Vision-Inducing Works." In *Intersections: Fantasy and Science Fiction*. Ed. George E. Slusser and Eric S. Rabkin. Carbondale: Southern Illinois UP, 1987. 97–106.

Cowper, Richard. *The Road to Corlay*. New York: Pocket, 1979.

Crowley, John. *Ægypt*. New York: Bantam, 1987.

———. *Engine Summer*. New York: Bantam, 1980.

———. "From Unthank to Glasgow and Back." *New York Times Book Review* 5 May 1985: 14–15.

———. *Little, Big*. New York: Bantam, 1981.

Culler, Jonathan. *On Deconstruction: Theory and Criticism after Structuralism*. Ithaca: Cornell UP, 1982.

de Camp, L. Sprague, and Fletcher Pratt. *The Compleat Enchanter: The Magical Misadventures of Harold Shea*, containing "The Roaring Trumpet" (1940), "The Mathematics of Magic" (1940), and "The Castle of Iron" (1941). New York: Ballantine, 1975.

———. *Wall of Serpents,* containing "The Wall of Serpents" (1953) and "The Green Magician" (1954). New York: Dell, 1979.

Delany, Samuel R. *The Einstein Intersection*. New York: Ace, 1967.

de Lint, Charles. *Moonheart*. New York: Ace, 1984.

Dickson, Gordon. *The Dragon and the George*. Garden City: Doubleday, 1976.

Donaldson, Stephen. "Epic Fantasy in the Modern World." Kent State University Library Occasional Papers, 2nd Series, No. 2. Kent, OH: Kent State Library, n.d.

Eastman, Max. *The Sense of Humor*. New York: Scribner's, 1922.

Elgin, Don D. *The Comedy of the Fantastic: Ecological Perspectives on the Fantasy Novel*. Contributions to the Study of Science Fiction and Fantasy, Number 15. Westport: Greenwood, 1985.

Elgin, Suzette Haden. *The Ozark Trilogy,* consisting of *Twelve Fair Kingdoms, The Grand Jubilee,* and *And Then There'll Be Fireworks*. Book Club Edition. Garden City: Doubleday, 1981.

Eliade, Mircea. *Rites and Symbols of Initiation: The Mysteries of Birth and Rebirth*. Trans. Willard R. Trask. New York: Harper, 1958.

Flieger, Verlyn. *Splintered Light: Logos and Language in Tolkien's World*. Grand Rapids: Eerdmans, 1983.

Forster, E. M. *Aspects of the Novel*. New York: Harcourt, 1927.

Frye, Northrop. *Anatomy of Criticism: Four Essays*. Princeton: Princeton UP, 1957.

———. *The Secular Scripture: A Study of the Structure of Romance*. Cambridge, MA: Harvard UP, 1976.

Garner, Alan. "A Bit More Practice." *The Times Literary Supplement* 6 June 1968. Rpt. in *The Cool Web: The Pattern of Children's Reading.* Ed. Margaret Meek, Aidan Warlow, and Griselda Barton. New York: Atheneum, 1978. 196–200.

———. *Elidor.* 1965; rpt. New York: Ballantine, 1981.

———. *The Moon of Gomrath.* 1963; rpt. New York: Ballantine, 1981.

———. *The Owl Service.* London: Collins, 1967.

———. *Red Shift.* London: Collins, 1973.

———. *The Weirdstone of Brisingamen.* 1960; rpt. New York: Ballantine, 1981.

Genette, Gérard. *Narrative Discourse: An Essay in Method.* Trans. Jane E. Lewin. Ithaca: Cornell UP, 1980.

Gerrold, David. *Moonstar Odyssey.* New York: Signet, 1977.

Grant, Patrick. "Tolkien: Archetype and Word." In *Tolkien: New Critical Perspectives.* Ed. Neil D. Isaacs and Rose A. Zimbardo. Lexington, KY: UP of Kentucky, 1981. 87–105.

Hamilton, Virginia. *Justice and Her Brothers.* New York: Greenwillow, 1978.

Hazel, Paul. *Undersea.* Boston: Little, 1982.

Heilbrun, Carolyn G. *Reinventing Womanhood.* New York: Norton, 1979.

Heinlein, Robert E. *Glory Road.* New York: Putnam's, 1964.

Helprin, Mark. *Winter's Tale.* New York: Harcourt, 1983.

Hume, Kathryn. *Fantasy and Mimesis: Responses to Reality in Western Literature.* New York: Methuen, 1984.

Ingelow, Jean. *Mopsa the Fairy.* London: Longmans, 1869. Rpt. in *A Christmas Carol by Charles Dickens; and Other Victorian Fairy Tales by John Ruskin, W. M. Thackeray, George MacDonald, and Jean Ingelow.* Selected by U. C. Knoepflmacher. New York: Bantam, 1983.

Irwin, W. R. *The Game of the Impossible: A Rhetoric of Fantasy.* Urbana: U of Illinois P, 1976.

Isaacs, Neil D., and Rose A. Zimbardo, eds. *Tolkien and the Critics: Essays on J. R. R. Tolkien's The Lord of the Rings.* Notre Dame: U of Notre Dame P, 1968.

Jackson, Rosemary. *Fantasy: The Literature of Subversion.* New York: Methuen, 1981.

Jacobs, Joseph. *English Folk and Fairy Tales.* 3rd ed. revised. New York: Putnam's, n.d.

Jameson, Fredric. "Magical Narrative: Romance as Genre." *New Literary History* 7:1 (Autumn 1975): 135–63.

———. "Postmodernism, or The Cultural Logic of Late Capitalism." *New Left Review* 146 (July-August 1984): 53–94.

———. "Science Fiction as a Spatial Genre: Generic Discontinuities and the Problem of Figuration in Vonda McIntyre's *The Exile Waiting.*" *Science-Fiction Studies* 14 (March 1987): 44–59.

Jaynes, Julian. *The Origin of Consciousness in the Breakdown of the Bicameral Mind.* Boston: Houghton, 1976.

Jones, Diana Wynne. *Archer's Goon.* New York: Greenwillow, 1984.

———. *Fire and Hemlock.* New York: Greenwillow, 1985.

———. "The Shape of the Narrative in *The Lord of the Rings.*" In *J. R. R. Tolkien: This Far Land.* Ed. Robert Giddings. London: Vision, 1983. 87–107.

———. *The Spell-Coats.* New York: Atheneum, 1979.

———. *The Time of the Ghost.* London: Macmillan, 1984.

Koestler, Arthur. *The Act of Creation*. New York: Macmillan, 1964.
———. "Humour and Wit." *Encyclopaedia Britannica: Macropaedia*, 1974.
Kress, Nancy. *Prince of the Morning Bells*. New York: Pocket, 1981.
Lakoff, George, and Mark Johnson. *Metaphors We Live By*. Chicago: U of Chicago P, 1980.
Laumer, Keith. *The Time Bender*. New York: Ace, 1981.
Le Guin, Ursula K. *City of Illusions*. New York: Ace, 1967.
———. *The Farthest Shore*. New York: Atheneum, 1972.
———. *The Language of the Night: Essays on Fantasy and Science Fiction*. Ed. Susan Wood. New York: Putnam's, 1979.
———. *The Left Hand of Darkness*. New York: Ace, 1969.
———. *Planet of Exile*. New York: Ace, 1966.
———. *Rocannon's World*. New York: Ace, 1966.
———. "Spike the Canon." *SFRA Newsletter* 169 (July/August 1989): 17–21.
———. *Tehanu: The Last Book of Earthsea*. New York: Atheneum, 1990.
———. *The Tombs of Atuan*. New York: Atheneum, 1971.
———. *A Wizard of Earthsea*. Berkeley: Parnassus, 1968.
Lewis, C. S. "De Descriptione Temporum." In *Selected Literary Essays*. Ed. Walter Hooper. Cambridge: Cambridge UP, 1969. 1–14.
———. *Of Other Worlds: Essays and Stories*. Ed. Walter Hooper. New York: Harcourt, 1966.
——— *Out of the Silent Planet*. London: Lane, 1938.
Lincoln, Bruce. *Emerging from the Chrysalis: Studies in Rituals of Women's Initiation*. Cambridge, MA: Harvard UP, 1981.
Lindholm, Megan. *Wizard of the Pigeons*. New York: Ace, 1986.
Longstreth, Richard. "Bernard Maybeck." In *Master Builders: A Guide to Famous American Architects*. Ed. Dianne Maddex. Washington: National Trust for Historic Preservation, 1985. 128–31.
Lundell, Torborg. "Gender-Related Biases in the Type and Motif Indexes of Aarne and Thompson." In *Fairy Tales and Society: Illusion, Allusion, and Paradigm*. Ed. Ruth B. Bottigheimer. Philadelphia: U of Pennsylvania P, 1986. 149–63.
MacAvoy, R. A. *Tea with the Black Dragon*. New York: Bantam, 1983.
MacDonald, George. *Phantastes: A Faerie Romance for Men and Women*. London: Smith, Elder, 1858. Rpt. in *Phantastes and Lilith*. Grand Rapids, MI: Eerdmans, 1964.
MacDonald, John D. *The Girl, the Gold Watch, and Everything*. Greenwich: Fawcett, 1962.
McKillip, Patricia A. *Riddle of Stars*, consisting of *The Riddle-Master of Hed* (1976), *Heir of Sea and Fire* (1977), and *Harpist in the Wind* (1979). Book Club Edition. Garden City: Doubleday, n.d.
Makkreel, Rudolph A. *Dilthey: Philosopher of the Human Studies*. Princeton: Princeton UP, 1975.
Manlove, C. N. *The Impulse of Fantasy Literature*. Kent, OH: The Kent State UP, 1983.
———. *Modern Fantasy: Five Studies*. Cambridge: Cambridge UP, 1975.
Meeker, Joseph. *The Comedy of Survival: Studies in Literary Ecology*. New York: Scribner's, 1974.
Millhauser, Steven. *From the Realm of Morpheus*. New York: Morrow, 1986.
Mobley, Jane. "Toward a Definition of Fantasy Fiction." *Extrapolation* 15 (1973–74): 117–28.

The National Cyclopedia of American Biography. New York: James T. White, 1932.

Nesbit, E[dith]. *Harding's Luck*. 1910. London: Benn, 1961.

——. *The House of Arden*. 1908. London: Dent, 1967.

——. *The Story of the Amulet*. 1907. New York: Looking Glass Library, n.d.

Norton, Andre. *The Beast Master*. New York: Harcourt, 1959.

——. *Catseye*. New York: Harcourt, 1961.

——. *Judgment on Janus*. New York: Harcourt, 1963.

——. "On Writing Fantasy." *The Book of Andre Norton*. New York: DAW, 1975. Rpt. in *Fantasists on Fantasy: A Collection of Critical Reflections*. Ed. Robert Boyer and Kenneth J. Zahorski. New York: Avon, 1984. 154–61.

——. *Year of the Unicorn*. New York: Ace, 1965.

Olsen, Lance. *Ellipse of Uncertainty: An Introduction to Postmodern Fantasy*. Contributions to the Study of Science Fiction and Fantasy, No. 26. New York: Greenwood, 1987.

Paxson, Diana. *Brisingamen*. New York: Berkley, 1984.

Peirce, Charles Sanders. *Collected Papers*. Ed. Charles Hartshorne and Paul Weiss. 6 vols. Cambridge, MA: Harvard UP, 1960.

Phelps, Ethel Johnston. *Tatterhood and Other Tales*. Old Westbury: The Feminist Press, 1978.

Prickett, Stephen. *Victorian Fantasy*. Bloomington: Indiana UP, 1979.

Propp, Vladimir. *Morphology of the Folktale*. Trans. Laurence Scott. 2nd ed. revised and ed. Louis A. Wagner. Austin: U of Texas P, 1968.

Rabkin, Eric S. *The Fantastic in Literature*. Princeton: Princeton UP, 1976.

Raffel, Burton. "*The Lord of the Rings* as Literature." In *Tolkien and the Critics*. Ed. Neil D. Isaacs and Rose A. Zimbardo. Notre Dame: U of Notre Dame P, 1968. 218–46.

Roessner, Michaela. *Walkabout Woman*. New York: Bantam, 1988.

Rosaldo, Michelle Zimbalist. "Women, Culture, and Society: A Theoretical Overview." In *Women, Culture, and Society*. Ed. Michelle Zimbalist Rosaldo and Louise Lamphere. Stanford: Stanford UP, 1974. 17–42.

Schmitz, James. *The Witches of Karres*. New York: Ace, 1966.

Scholes, Robert. *Fabulation and Metafiction*. Urbana: U of Illinois P, 1979.

——. *Structuralism in Literature: An Introduction*. New Haven: Yale UP, 1974.

Shinn, Thelma J. *Worlds within Women: Myth and Mythmaking in Fantastic Literature by Women*. Contributions to the Study of Science Fiction and Fantasy, Number 22. Westport: Greenwood, 1986.

Shippey, T. A. *The Road to Middle-Earth*. Boston: Houghton, 1983.

Siebers, Tobin. *The Romantic Fantastic*. Ithaca: Cornell UP, 1984.

Singal, Daniel Joseph. "Towards a Definition of American Modernism." *American Quarterly* 39 (Spring 1987): 7–26.

Spacks, Patricia Meyer. *The Female Imagination*. NY: Knopf, 1975.

Spivack, Charlotte. *Merlin's Daughters: Contemporary Women Writers of Fantasy*. Contributions to the Study of Science Fiction and Fantasy, Number 23. Westport: Greenwood, 1987.

Stasheff, Christopher. *The Warlock in Spite of Himself*. New York: Ace, 1969.

Stone, Kay. "Things Walt Disney Never Told Us." In *Women and Folklore: Images and Genres*. Ed. Claire R. Farrer. Prospect Heights: Waveland, 1975. 42–50.

Suvin, Darko. *Metamorphoses of Science Fiction: On the Poetics and History of a Literary Genre*. New Haven: Yale UP, 1979.

Swinfen, Ann. *In Defense of Fantasy: A Study of the Genre in English and American Literature since 1945.* London: Routledge, 1984.

Tepper, Sheri S. *Marianne, the Magus, and the Manticore.* New York: Ace, 1985.

Timmerman, John H. *Other Worlds: The Fantasy Genre.* Bowling Green: Bowling Green U Popular Press, 1983.

Todorov, Tzvetan. *The Fantastic: A Structural Approach to a Literary Genre.* Trans. Richard Howard. Ithaca: Cornell UP, 1975.

———. *Mikhail Bakhtin: The Dialogical Principle.* Trans. Wlad Godzich. Theory and History of Literature, Number 13. Minneapolis: U of Minnesota P, 1984.

Tolkien, J. R. R. "*Beowulf*: The Monsters and the Critics." *Proceedings of the British Academy XXII.* Oxford: Oxford UP, 1937. Rpt. in *An Anthology of Beowulf Criticism.* Ed. Lewis E. Nicholson. South Bend: U of Notre Dame P, 1963. 51–103.

———. *The Lord of the Rings.* Revised ed. 3 vols.: *The Fellowship of the Ring, The Two Towers,* and *The Return of the King.* Boston: Houghton, 1967.

———. "On Fairy-Stories." In *Tree and Leaf.* Boston: Houghton, 1965. 3–84.

Tymn, Marshall B., Kenneth J. Zahorski, and Robert H. Boyer. *Fantasy Literature: A Core Collection and Reference Guide.* New York: Bowker, 1979.

Updike, John. *The Witches of Eastwick.* New York: Knopf, 1984.

van Gennep, Arnold. *The Rites of Passage.* Trans. Monika B. Vizedom and Gabrielle L. Caffee. Chicago: U of Chicago P, 1960.

Waugh, Patricia. *Metafiction: The Theory and Practice of Self-Conscious Fiction.* New York: Methuen, 1984.

White, Hayden. *The Content of the Form: Narrative Discourse and Historical Representation.* Baltimore: The Johns Hopkins UP, 1987.

White, T. H. *The Sword in the Stone.* London: Collins, 1938.

Wilde, Alan. *Horizons of Assent: Modernism, Postmodernism, and the Ironic Imagination.* Baltimore: The Johns Hopkins UP, 1981.

Willard, Nancy. *Things Invisible to See.* New York: Knopf, 1985.

Wilson, Edmund. *Axel's Castle: A Study in the Imaginative Literature of 1870–1930.* New York: Scribner's, 1931.

———. "Oo, Those Awful Orcs." *The Nation* 14 April 1956: 312–14. Rpt. in *The Bit between My Teeth: A Literary Chronicle of 1950–1965.* New York: Farrar, 1965. 326–32.

Wintle, Justin, and Emma Fisher. *The Pied Pipers: Interviews with the Influential Creators of Children's Literature.* New York: Paddington, 1974.

Wolfe, Gary K. *Critical Terms for Science Fiction and Fantasy: A Glossary and Guide to Scholarship.* Westport: Greenwood, 1986.

———. *The Known and the Unknown: The Iconography of Science Fiction.* Kent, OH: The Kent State UP, 1979.

Wolfe, Gene. *The Book of the New Sun,* consisting of *The Shadow of the Torturer* (New York: Timescape, 1980), *The Claw of the Conciliator* (New York: Timescape, 1981), *The Sword of the Lictor* (New York: Timescape, 1981), and *The Citadel of the Autarch* (New York: Timescape, 1983).

———. *The Urth of the New Sun.* New York: TOR, 1987.

Woolf, Virginia. *Orlando: A Biography.* New York: Harcourt, 1928.

Wrightson, Patricia. *The Dark Bright Water.* New York: Atheneum, 1979.

———. *The Ice Is Coming.* New York: Atheneum, 1977.

Young, David, and Keith Hollaman, eds. *Magic Realist Fiction: An Anthology.* New York: Longman, 1984.

Zelazny, Roger. *Creatures of Light and Darkness.* Garden City: Doubleday, 1969.

———. *Lord of Light.* Garden City: Doubleday, 1967.

Index

BRIAN ATTEBERY is Associate Professor of English at Idaho State University and the author of *The Fantasy Tradition in American Literature,* one of the pioneering works in the field of fantasy scholarship. He was Scholar Guest of Honor at the 1988 meeting of the Mythopoeic Society and in 1991 was given the Distinguished Scholarship Award by the International Association for the Fantastic in the Arts.